A WINTER STREAM IN FINNISH LAPLAND

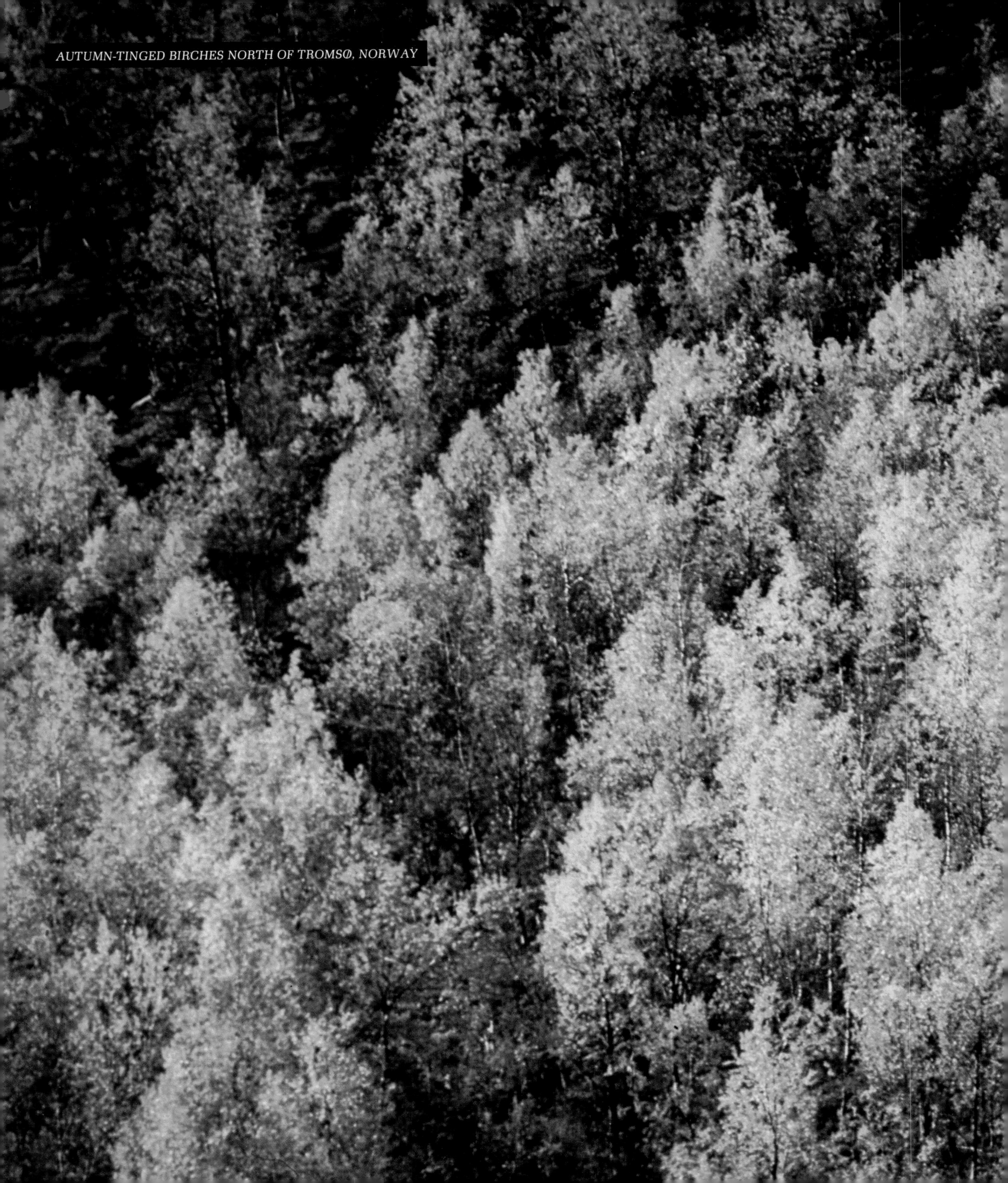

AUTUMN-TINGED BIRCHES NORTH OF TROMSØ, NORWAY

REINDEER MIGRATING ACROSS A MOUNTAIN SLOPE

SWEDEN'S LILLA LULEÅ RIVER IN THE DRY SUMMER SEASON

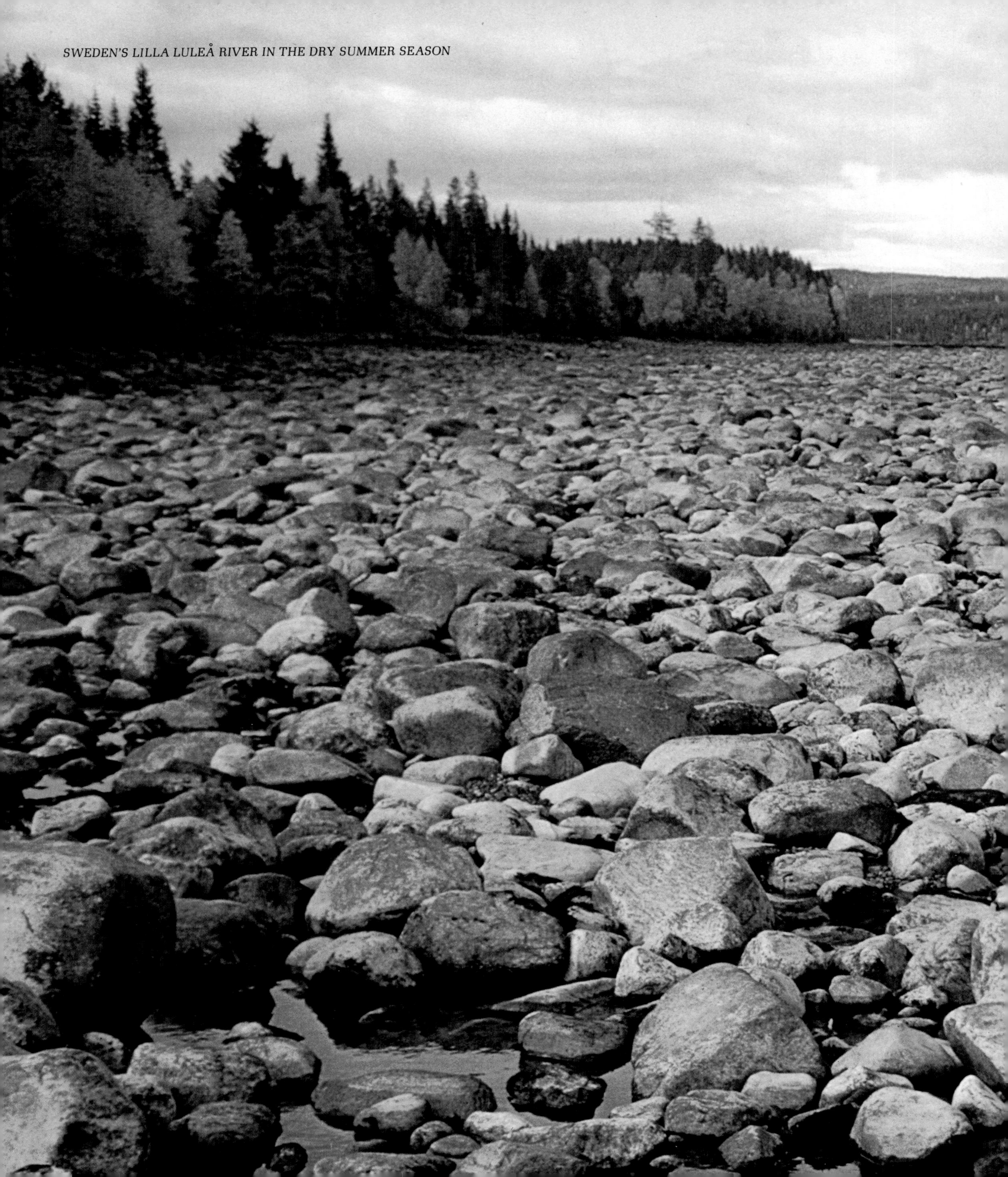

STORM CLOUDS OVER SWEDISH LAPLAND

A BROWN BEAR IN SWEDEN'S SAREK NATIONAL PARK

MOUNTAIN BACKDROP TO FINNISH LAPLAND'S LAKE KILPISJARVI

LIFE NATURE LIBRARY
LIFE SCIENCE LIBRARY
GREAT AGES OF MAN
FOODS OF THE WORLD
TIME-LIFE LIBRARY OF ART
LIFE LIBRARY OF PHOTOGRAPHY
THE EMERGENCE OF MAN
THE OLD WEST
THE ART OF SEWING

LAPLAND

THE WORLD'S WILD PLACES/TIME-LIFE BOOKS/AMSTERDAM

BY WALTER MARSDEN
AND THE EDITORS OF TIME-LIFE BOOKS

THE WORLD'S WILD PLACES

Editorial Staff for *Lapland*:
EUROPEAN EDITOR: Dale Brown
Deputy Editor: Christopher Farman
Picture Editor: Pamela Marke
Design Consultant: Louis Klein
Staff Writers:
Michael Brown, Windsor Chorlton,
Dan Freeman, Heather Sherlock
Art Director: Graham Davis
Designer: Joyce Mason
Picture Researcher: Margrite Prah
Picture Assistant: Cathy Doxat-Pratt
Editorial Researcher: Vanessa Kramer
Editorial Assistant: Ellen Brush
Copy Staff: Julia West

Consultants
Botany: Christopher Grey-Wilson, Phyllis Edwards
Geology: Dr. Clifford Embleton, Dr. Peter Stubbs
Herpetology: David Ball
Icthyology: Alwyne Wheeler
Meteorology: Lt. Cdr. Bruce Doxat-Pratt
Invertebrates: Michael Tweedie
Ornithology: Dr. P. J. K. Burton
Zoology: Dr. P. J. K. Burton

The captions and text of the picture essays were
written by the staff of Time-Life Books.

Valuable assistance was given in the preparation of
this volume by the following Time-Life correspondents:
Christensen Dag, Oslo; Mary Johnson, Stockholm;
Lance Keyworth, Helsinki and Felix Rosenthal,
Moscow.

Published by Time-Life International (Nederland) B.V.
5 Ottho Heldringstraat, Amsterdam 18.

The Author:
Walter Marsden, a journalist and writer,
has travelled extensively in Europe. His
interest in Lapland arose from his fasci-
nation with lemmings, about which he
has written a classic study, *The Lemming
Year*. He has also written three novels
and a number of travel books, one of
them on the Rhineland.

The Book Consultant:
Dr. Ethel John Lindgren, a former Cambridge University lecturer in social an-
thropology, has maintained a life-long
interest in reindeer. Before the Second
World War she led three expeditions to
north-west Manchuria to study the Tun-
gus, a reindeer-breeding people, and she
is currently Honorary Secretary of the
Reindeer Council of the United Kingdom.
She has travelled widely in Swedish
Lapland.

The Cover: The smooth waters of the
river Kauhajoki, in the far north of
Finnish Lapland, perfectly reflect the
roseate hues of a summer midnight sky.

Contents

The Roof of Europe

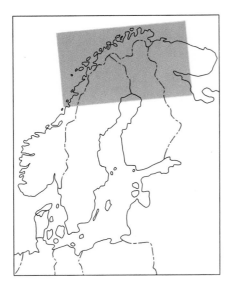

Lying almost totally within the Arctic Circle, Lapland (shaded rectangle above) stretches across northern regions of Norway, Sweden and Finland and touches the Kola peninsula of Russia. The landscape, an area of about 100,000 square miles shown in the topographical map at right, bears the indelible imprint of the last Ice Age. To the west are high, glaciated mountains (brown) and a coastline heavily indented with fjords. East of these mountains is an undulating, tundra-like plateau (yellow) chequered with bogs (tufts) and traversed by rivers (blue). Round its edges and reaching into the valleys are birch and coniferous forests, shown in dark green.

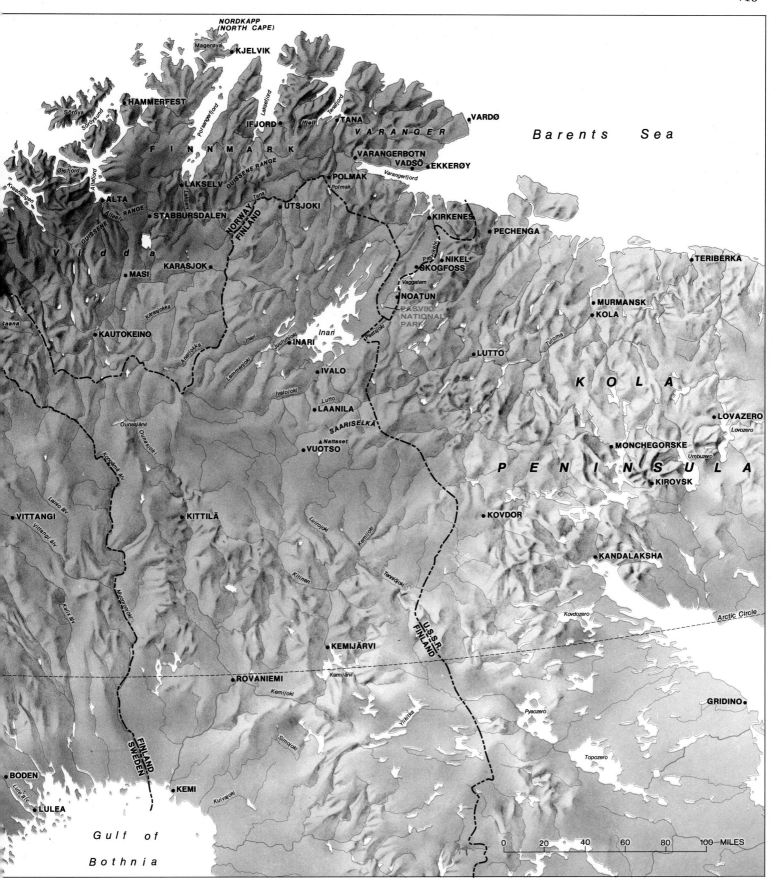

1/ Land of the Reindeer

*There is a deep silence in Lapland, a silence only
occasionally emphasized, rather than broken, by the
faint sighing of the wind, or the whisper of far
waters.*   R. P. LISTER/ *A JOURNEY IN LAPLAND*

The aeroplane left Oslo in the gathering dusk of a cloudy summer
evening, heading north towards Lapland on a journey of more than a
thousand miles, farther than if we had been going from Oslo to Milan.
Gradually the light dimmed—but darkness did not fall. Instead, the sun
began to rise again from below the horizon, the clouds thinned and by
midnight, well north of the Arctic Circle, we were in a gloriously clear
sky, blue above, rosy below. We flew high over a huge glacier and then
an awesome landscape of snow-capped peaks and stark ridges that
stretched as far as I could see: the mountains of Lapland under the
midnight sun.

Looking for Lapland on a map can be a confusing business, for it is
neither a nation-state nor the province of a single country. It is the
homeland of the Lapps, a people whose boundaries have been set by the
instinctive migrations of their reindeer herds rather than by the decrees
of governments. The Lapps have lived on the northernmost fringes of
Europe since before recorded history, and there are now in the region
of 30,000 of them, spread over an area that extends from the Atlantic
coast of Norway to the White Sea and from the Arctic Ocean to well
south of the Arctic Circle.

For practical reasons I had decided to confine my present journeying
to that part of Lapland lying within the boundaries of Norway, Sweden
and Finland above the Arctic Circle. "Confine" is perhaps a misleading

word, for the area I planned to visit comprises 100,000 square miles of mountains, lakes, forests, bogs and uplands, and it is the largest wilderness in western Europe. The landscape is primeval and, as I knew from experience, traversing it can be difficult and even dangerous.

Maps of Lapland are often inaccurate, very few paths thread the uplands, and barely a frail bridge spans torrents so cold that even mosses cannot grow near by. Yet in summer the hot air quivers over the moors and valleys and mosquitoes, gnats and gadflies swarm across the lowlands, driving reindeer to seek the insect-free sanctuary of the mountain slopes. But the traveller who explores these cold and enticing uplands must be prepared for rainstorms that come suddenly and can last for several days, reducing visibility to a few yards, swelling the glacier brooks into foaming cataracts and churning the ground into a knee-depth quagmire. It is easy to get lost in Lapland. Outside the towns there are few places in which the population density is more than one or two persons to the square mile and many in which it is less, so that it is possible to wander for days entirely at the mercy of this vast and capricious wilderness.

But if the challenges are great, the rewards for overcoming them are exceptional. Lapland's craggy coasts and multitudinous marshes are summer breeding grounds for birds from Europe, Asia and Africa; the unpolluted waters of its countless lakes and rivers abound with fish and other aquatic creatures; its steep mountain slopes and sprawling conifer forests harbour the bear, the wolf, the lynx and the wolverine—animals that have already passed into history or legend in most other parts of the European continent.

It may seem paradoxical that an area lying in a latitude farther north even than the mighty glaciers of southern Greenland should provide a haven for wildlife. But the climate, like so much else in Lapland, is unusual. The North Atlantic Drift brings tropical waters from the Gulf of Mexico to Lapland's shores, raising the temperature of the moist westerly and south-westerly Atlantic winds. As a result, Lapland is warmer than any other region so far north and has the longest ice-free coast in the polar world. Even in January the temperature of north-west Lapland is about 60° F. higher than the average for the latitude, and the west coast is actually slightly warmer than Oslo.

Farther east, however, the climate begins to change. The mountains along the Norwegian/Swedish frontier cause the Atlantic airstreams to rise, cool, and give off their moisture as rain or snow. Hence western Lapland has a precipitation of approximately 40 inches a year, much of it falling in autumn and early winter. East of the mountains the winds sink again but are here relatively dry, with less rainfall and snow. Instead of the oceanic climate experienced in the west, there is a more continental climate, with greater extremes of temperature, the summers hot and dry, the winters extremely cold.

In spite of a relatively mild arctic climate, however, Lapland is predominantly a winter land. Autumn arrives by September, with temperatures between 40° F. and 32° F., and from early October to the end of April, when the spring thaw begins, snow and ice dominate the landscape. February is the coldest month, with temperatures ranging from 8° F. to 0° F., and in some places, especially on the fells, the thermometer can fall below —14° F. But summer, when it finally arrives at the end of May, can reach Mediterranean intensity. Karasjok, on the barren, tundra-like plateau known as the *vidda*, has experienced a winter temperature of —59° F., the lowest recorded in north Norway, yet I have been there in July when the temperature stayed at 86° F.

Even more impressive than Lapland's sweltering summer heat is the extraordinary phenomenon known as the midnight sun. It had lighted the path of our flight all the way north from the Arctic Circle and it was still softly radiating through the hazy July sky when we stepped off the aircraft in the early hours of the morning. In one sense, of course, midnight sun is a misnomer: how can there be midnight when there is no darkness? But the term has become almost synonymous with summer in the Arctic. Because of the angle at which the earth's axis is tilted in its orbit around the sun, there are periods of varying length in summer north of the Arctic Circle when the sun does not set. On the Circle there is only one day each year, the summer solstice, which has continuous daylight for 24 hours. Closer to the North Pole, the period of continuous daylight increases until at the pole itself the sun remains above the horizon for roughly six months of the year. During the other six months, however, there is almost continuous darkness as the sun seems to move away south. In northernmost Lapland the period of continuous daylight lasts from mid-May to late July. Then the days begin to shorten until November when the sun disappears below the horizon for two months.

Because summer is so brief, the midnight sun is essential to Lapland's flora and wildlife. Plants are able to thrive in the light they receive for 24 hours a day and all animals depend, directly or indirectly, upon plants. Herbivores, such as lemmings, eat the plants, while carnivores, like the arctic fox, eat the herbivores. The luxuriance of summer plant growth is startling. In the valleys the air is laden with the scent of

Arctic fox cubs prowl near their summer den. Food is brought by the parents, but by autumn the cubs will be able to do their own hunting.

globe flower and goldenrod and the fells are carpeted with red arctic heather and pink wild azalea.

There is, nevertheless, far less variety than in temperate zones, for only comparatively few plant species have been able to adapt to the rigours of arctic living. Most of those that have adapted huddle close to the ground: they are characterized by their small size and compact stature in the form of cushions, rosettes or tufts, all signs of their unceasing struggle against cold, scant or acid soil, and even drought and desiccation. Various survival techniques are resorted to. The white-petalled *Diapensia*, for example, puts down a strong, probing tap-root that enables it to exist even on ridges parched by drying winds and swept almost clear of snow in winter. Some plants withstand prolonged drought by developing small, leathery leaves or by having densely matted hairs over their leaves and stems, thus reducing evaporation. Others, including the Lapland rose, utilize both devices.

A few brave species, such as the tiny dwarf sorrel, make a fleeting annual appearance, but most plants are perennials, lying dormant in winter under the protective covering of the snow and flowering in spring or summer. Nothing, however, is certain in this changeable land and there may be seasons when, in spite of the long winter under the snow, conditions do not permit flowering.

Another characteristic arctic phenomenon is Lapland's relatively small number of insect species, which means that plants can rely upon insect pollination only to a limited extent. Some, like the birch, willow and juniper, are wind-pollinated. Others, including the bilberry, alpine bearberry and blue mountain heath, are self-pollinating. In fact, most plants produce abundant seeds, but the severe climate can prevent germination, and so survival of the species is guaranteed by a process known as vegetative reproduction. Occurring independently of fertilization, it enables a plant to develop stems, shoots or bulbils that become detached and subsequently grow into new plants. This form of reproduction is usually successful because it can take place at lower temperatures and over a shorter period than the sexual process.

I spent the first few days in Lapland within easy reach of the mountains. For the time being, however, I resisted the lure of their windy slopes and ice-clad summits because I had a rare opportunity of joining some Lapp reindeer herders at their summer camp in the far north, close to the Arctic Ocean. The Lapps once depended upon their reindeer as closely as the Bedouin depend upon their camels; but today there are no more than 5,000 Lapps who still derive their main income from reindeer, and

A member of the dogwood family, the cornelian cherry is a tough-barked shrub that grows on Lapland's highland slopes. Its small, yellow flowers (above) bloom in spring and last for about six weeks, followed in autumn by clusters of red, acid berries (right).

of these only a tiny majority still follow the ancient nomadic traditions of their ancestors.

But who were the Lapps' ancestors and whence did they originate? Scholars have been trying to solve these questions ever since the Roman historian, Tacitus, wrote almost 2,000 years ago of the Fenni, an "extraordinarily wild and horribly poor" tribe that lived on the north-eastern fringes of the great Germanic plains. Most authorities have identified the Fenni with the Lapps, but speculation about the Lapps' earliest origins continues. A popular theory is that Lapps and Finns once shared a common Asiatic homeland and that the Lapps began a long migration that led them eventually to Finland and Scandinavia, where they arrived ahead of the Finns. Exponents of this theory point to the fact that both the Finnish and Lapp tongues belong to the Finno-Ugric group and they maintain that the Lapps derived their distinctive physical characteristics —short stature, rather pear-shaped face, darkish hair and olive complexion—from mingling with the peoples who were already in northern Europe when they arrived.

Others believe that the Lapps have always lived in their present homeland and that they may once have spoken an entirely different language that became modified or replaced by Finnish. Indeed, some Lapps prefer to be known as Same or Sameh, since the name "Lapp" is thought to derive from an archaic Finnish word meaning "banished". According

Reindeer featured prominently in the religious rites as well as the everyday life of the early Lapps. This woodcut, taken from Johannes Schefferus's book, The History of the Lapps, published in 1673, shows a man bowing before a sacred stone image surrounded by inter-locked reindeer antlers. Schefferus, an Alsatian philologist who made an intensive study of Lapp customs, described in his book how the antlers were taken from ritually slaughtered animals by the priest who "then anoints the stone with the fat and blood, and places the horns behind it".

to the Swedish Lapp author, Johan Turi, "No one has ever heard that the Lapps came to this land from any other place. From the very earliest times they have been here in Lapland; and when, in the beginning, the Lapps lived by the sea coast, there was not a single other person." Turi writes from the viewpoint of a poet and patriot rather than a scientist, but there are experts who share his view. If it is correct, then the Lapps were living in Lapland some 8,000 years ago, for stone implements of that age have been discovered on the coast of north Norway.

There is little doubt that from earliest times the life of the Lapps was bound up with reindeer, although it is not known for certain when they turned to herding as a supplement to hunting. As early as the year A.D. 892 the Norwegian chieftain, Ohthere, informed King Alfred of Wessex that the Lapps were hunters and fishers who also captured reindeer. But as the great herds of wild reindeer grew less plentiful and economic, social and political pressures increased, hunting declined in importance and, from about the 16th Century, four separate occupational groups began to emerge among the Lapps.

There were Mountain Lapps, who tended semi-wild reindeer herds, moving with them on the long migrations between winter foraging in the forests or on the plateau lands and summer grazing ranges in the mountains or near the coast; there were Forest Lapps, who sometimes added agriculture to reindeer breeding; and there were Sea and River Lapps, whose main means of livelihood was fishing. In the past all these groups were more or less nomadic, but nowadays the Forest Lapps undertake only short migrations with their animals, which are tamer and are formed into smaller herds than those of the Mountain Lapps. The Sea and River Lapps lead settled lives and frequently are no longer even fishermen. It is among the Mountain Lapps alone that the old ways still persist. They are western Europe's last wilderness folk, and it was for this reason that I made the visit to a summer reindeer camp my immediate priority.

After travelling north-east by air and road, I completed the journey on foot. Since my Lapp friends do not want their isolation penetrated, I am unable to give the exact location of their camp. I can only say that I found it a few miles from the arctic coast of north Norway. Four conical tents that looked like Red Indian tepees were set on an isolated bluff that overlooked a broad valley. Scattered alders and willows marked the course of a stream, and sparse birches, typically stunted and distorted by the elements, grew in the shadow of the gaunt fells that rose on either side. Northwards the fells dropped away sharply to a coastal plain that stretched for something like two miles to the Arctic Ocean.

It is nowadays unusual for Lapps to live in tents at their summer camps, but out of the pride for their ancestors the seven men in this group refused to build permanent turf huts or wooden cabins. They had made a few sensible concessions. The tent covering was not birch-bark, as in the past, but sacking stretched over a dozen poles with forked upper ends; they used thread instead of reindeer sinews; and they had left behind the women and children—the latter for schooling. Wherever possible, however, they clung to tradition. Domesticated pack-reindeer were grazing at the foot of the bluff, and carefully propped up among the birches were the boat-shaped sledges, or *pulka*, the Lapps had used on their 200-mile trek across the snow, a trek that had lasted from the middle of April until the first week in May.

Although the colourful Lapp costume is becoming less common, everyone in this group was traditionally dressed. A blue tunic, much decorated with red, blue and yellow strips of felt, reached below the knees and was worn with narrow trousers and a broad leather belt from which dangled a sheathed knife. On his feet, each man wore heel-less working boots turned up at the toe and on his head a cushion-like cap of dark felt with four stuffed, protruding corners.

I learned later that none of the group wore socks—and with good reason. It is impossible, even in summer and with good boots on, to keep one's feet dry all day among the bogs and brooks of the vidda. Socks simply become wet, cold and uncomfortable. The traditional Lapp remedy is to pack their boots with a fine sedge, picked on the edge of the marshes. Beaten, dried and rolled for storage, it remains warm and comfortable in the wettest conditions. During a halt, the sedge is removed, impaled on a forked twig and held over a fire, drying in a few minutes. But putting it back in the boots is a work of art. The sedge must be rubbed and teased out, folded round the fist and then shoved into the boots. Once re-inserted, the sedge has to be arranged to the correct thickness and consistency so that there are no lumps. Unfortunately, I was never able to master the technique.

The Lapps had travelled with a herd of some 700 reindeer, but before I arrived most of the animals had been swum across to an island and the hundred or so that remained in the area of the camp were widely scattered. In fact, on the first day I saw only four reindeer. Three of them—a bull, a cow and a calf—came out of a birch thicket and then speedily retreated. The fourth, another bull, was not so shy and walked tantalizingly ahead of me for several yards. Little larger than a donkey and loping along on seemingly oversized hoofs, the reindeer is not the most prepossessing animal at the best of times—and this was not the best of times. The bull's greyish coat was being shed in shaggy mats as the new, reddish-brown hair grew; shreds of velvet hung down from the antlers and the white breeches on its hindquarters were decidedly tattered.

The reindeer rounded a boulder a moment after I photographed it, but by the time I had reached the same spot it was nowhere to be seen. Reindeer have an uncanny knack of vanishing even in the barest land- scape and, although the Lapps can point them out a mile away, it was my experience that they blend into almost any background. They are also adept at making the most of their environment, an ability that has enabled them to survive in Scandinavia throughout the 10,000 years since the glaciers of the last Ice Age receded northwards. Entirely herbivorous, the reindeer sustain themselves during Lapland's harsh winters by digging down through the snow with their front hoofs for so-called reindeer moss. This "moss" is actually lichen, many species of which belong to the genus *Cladonia*, and it grows abundantly in Lap- land. Ranging in colour from the yellow of old ivory to the speckled white of knopped wool yarn, the lichens are not only pretty but also display an amazing survival capacity. They are able to withstand extremes of heat and cold and can live for up to 4,500 years.

Towards the end of winter, thawing and sudden freezing can form tough ice-crusts over the snow and the reindeer start migrating to fresh pastures in the mountains or on the coast, supervised by their herders. The calves are born in May, often during the migration, and the herds must be halted for a couple of days at a time. Although there is grazing along the route, the summer heat and the insect pests soon make inland feeding unpleasant and the animals long to reach their new pastures as quickly as possible. There, in the foothills, along the coast and on the islands the reindeer roam freely until the night frosts of August signal a return to winter feeding grounds.

Having grown their glossy new coats and rubbed or threshed the velvet from their gleaming, newly-matured antlers, the bulls are at their most imposing by mid-September, and it is then that they start rounding up harems for the October rut. The antlers of reindeer can be magnifi- cent, and a pair may number 25 points. Size of antlers and strength determines an animal's status in the herd, and during rutting there are often prolonged tussles between rival bulls. Instead of goring each other they engage, heads down, in pushing contests and occasionally the

During the summer months in Lapland, daylight lasts around the clock. Even at midnight (right) the sun hovers above the horizon, playing havoc with the body's sense of time. In contrast are the twilight months of winter when the sun is never seen (below). From just below the horizon it casts a dim glow in the sky and at midday is far less bright than a summer midnight.

MID-WINTER'S DAY JUST PAST NOON, FINNISH LAPLAND

LATE AFTERNOON IN THE SPRING, NORWEGIAN LAPLAND

NEAR MIDNIGHT IN MID-SUMMER, FINNISH LAPLAND

antlers lock together so tightly that the animals are unable to free themselves and starve to death.

At the time of the rut the bulls indulge in more antler threshing, this time as part of the courtship display. But their lordly domination is short-lived, for the rut is a strenuous time, leaving the bulls exhausted and emaciated. After rutting they also shed their antlers until May, whereas non-pregnant females and gelded males retain these important status symbols until March or April. In common with the caribou, the wild reindeer of North America, the European and Asian reindeer are the only members of the deer family in which both sexes are horned. Pregnant cows do not normally shed their antlers until after they have given birth in May or June. During the vulnerable period just prior to giving birth, therefore, the females are accorded greatest deference, ensuring access to scarce lichen if necessary.

There was much more herding in progress than I realized at first. The reindeer had to be discouraged from making off across the fells and every few days they were rounded up by dogs the Lapps had brought with them—highly-skilled herding animals of mixed breed, but usually resembling the spitz. The Lapps were also on the look-out for young calves that did not yet have ownership notches cut in their ears; whenever these were discovered, they were lassoed and the appropriate ear-notches made with a hunting-knife.

In summer the chief creatures to be feared, especially by the calves and sick animals, are red foxes, ravens and eagles. The eagle will often shadow a pregnant female when it leaves the herd to give birth, perching near by when the cow settles in some isolated spot and swooping the moment its labour is over. Some reindeer-mothers flee at this point, leaving their defenceless offspring to their fate.

The vigilance of the herdsmen and the deadliness of the traps that they set give the reindeer some protection against predators, but little can be done to relieve the suffering inflicted on them by insects. I soon discovered for myself how vicious and persistent these can be. Wandering through some marshy ground near the camp soon after my arrival, I came across a patch of cloudberries, their delicate white flower heads looking like a flock of butterflies at rest. But as soon as I stopped to photograph them I was enveloped by mosquitoes. My hands were black with them and they covered my forehead, getting into my eyes and nose. When I opened my mouth in a vain expostulation, they eagerly entered and one of them irritated my throat for several minutes. I hastily set off, stamping my feet and flapping my arms, and eventually left most of the mosquitoes behind. Some blackflies, however, managed to find a route down from my ankles under the tongue of each boot and they feasted contentedly on my feet while others worked their way down my neck as far as my shoulder blades.

Mosquitoes and blackflies are just two of the insects that bother reindeer and during particularly bad summers it is not unknown for animals to spend so much time evading their tormentors that they are unable to eat and actually starve to death. The worst of these scourges are the nose botfly and the warble fly, which are both entirely dependent on the reindeer for completion of their life cycles. The nose botfly deposits its larvae live in the reindeer's nostrils. From here the larvae migrate to the sinuses, and by the following summer the animal's irritation is so great that it coughs, snorts and sneezes them on to the ground, where they pupate and then set the cycle in motion again. The reindeer try to keep their heads down among the herbage, but sooner or later the botflies will find a chance to attack.

The large, noisy warble fly lays its eggs on the reindeer's back or haunches and the reindeer, by licking, transfers them to its mouth, where the eggs hatch out. The larvae then pass down the digestive tract and are brought by the blood to lie under the skin of the reindeer's back, emerging the following summer through large sores and falling to the ground. Here, like the botfly larvae, they pupate and the whole grim process is repeated. No amount of stamping or skin-twitching deters the warble flies and one reindeer may become infested with hundreds of larvae. The Lapps call these insect pests their best herders, for to avoid them the reindeer move higher up the slopes where the grasses are more succulent. Sometimes the reindeer stand on a patch of snow, or even a glacier if there is one, where the cold air deters most of their oppressors. But the reindeer have to leave their refuge to graze and then they are again open to attack, even if considerably less so at the higher altitudes.

Reindeer meat formed the bulk of our diet in camp and, although there was no danger of the meat being infected, the thought of the reindeer playing host to their obnoxious parasites did little at first to improve my appetite. But after my qualms had passed I grew to like reindeer meat, which the Lapps boiled in a pot suspended over a fire by a chain dangling from a tripod of poles. I found it much more difficult to acquire a taste for some of the other culinary items enjoyed by the Lapps. Trudging up a hillside with the one Lapp in camp who was able to speak some English, I noticed a small brown plant growing among the heather, its fronds edged with ferocious-looking spines. In fact, the spines turned out to be blunt and my companion had no difficulty in pulling up the plant, trimming off a piece and munching it. Not to be outdone, I also took a piece and bit into it. But it was so bitter that I chewed only once before spitting it out. Then I saw that the Lapp, too, had spat his out. He laughed and admitted that it tasted better when boiled. Such was my introduction to "Icelandic" lichen, or bread moss, the best-known traditional vegetable food of the Lapps.

The next item on our gastronomic tour was angelica. My companion tore off several tall stems, peeled away the skin with his knife and began to eat the greenish pith underneath, offering me some as he chewed. It is supposed to taste like asparagus, but I found it inedible, perhaps because angelica is a delicacy of spring rather than summer and the stem had already become woody. The Lapp was undeterred, however, and went on munching happily while he explained that at one time his people had used angelica as a tobacco substitute as well as for food. He also had a gourmet's passion for the leaves of mountain sorrel which, he assured me, tasted like spinach when they were cooked, and in their raw state were ideal "for cleaning and refreshing the mouth". He tried hard to find some, but I cannot say that I was sorry when he abandoned the search and we headed back to rejoin his friends for the evening meal of reindeer meat.

As we passed one of the birch thickets that grew near the camp we heard a faint rustling and suddenly a red fox emerged from the undergrowth and bounded away. It was much larger than any I had seen outside Lapland, providing an impressive example of adaptation to arctic conditions. A big animal loses proportionately less body heat than a small one, and so, unlike plants, which tend to meet difficulties by remaining small, the animals of the north fare best by growing larger than their southern relatives. Northern species also have much more rounded heads and thickly-set physiques, since protruding parts, such as ears, tails, legs, muzzles and bills are subject to rapid heat loss.

Thick fur or plumage is another distinctive feature of all polar creatures. Even the pads of the arctic fox and the arctic hare are covered with fur, and the ptarmigan and the snowy owl, which are among the few bird species to remain in Lapland throughout the winter, have densely-feathered legs and toes. So effective is the fur insulation of large mammals that, from the size of the fox upwards, they are able to maintain their normal body temperatures without an increase in metabolism even when the air temperature falls to —20°F. But the fur of small mammals has to be thin enough to allow freedom of movement and its insulating power is therefore less effective than that of the fur on larger species. For animals such as the lemming and the vole this means winters spent in warm burrows under the snow. Particularly useful to these smaller species is the thick layer of fat that starts to accumulate beneath the skin in autumn and disappears again in spring. As well as providing extra protection against the cold, it serves as a reservoir of energy that can be tapped when food is difficult to come by.

I spent five days with the Lapps and during that time they worked almost ceaselessly among the reindeer scattered around the camp, recovering strays, ear-marking calves, watching for predators. But the busiest and most exciting time of the year is the round-up that follows the autumn rut. The animals are driven into corrals, where interlopers from other herds are sorted, calves that missed the earlier ear-marking are notched, and bulls no longer required for breeding are set aside for slaughter or castration. Animals selected for slaughter are stunned by a skilful blow to the back of the skull and then killed with a knife-thrust to the heart. Castration is usually performed with special forceps, although Lapps with good teeth effect the operation by biting, insisting that the animals make a quicker recovery when this traditional, if somewhat unpleasant, method is used.

Although reindeer are generally docile and timid, they gallop wildly around the corrals to avoid the lasso and may resist violently when captured. This can lead to some rough treatment by the herdsmen, resulting sometimes in injury to the animal, and the men, even though they have trained since boyhood to use the lasso, are occasionally scratched and bruised by the tossing antlers. But at last the work of the round-up is completed and there is time for the men to relax for a brew-up and a smoke before resuming the migration to the winter quarters.

As I said goodbye to my friends at the summer camp, I recalled Tacitus's reluctant admiration for their early ancestors, the Fenni. It was the Fenni's belief, he wrote, "that in some manner they are happier than those who sweat out their lives in the field and wear out their strength in houses, trafficking with their own fortunes and that of others. Careless towards both men and gods, they have achieved the most difficult thing of all: they have ceased to feel the harrying of men's desires".

Camouflage for All Seasons

Hunting or foraging the year round on the broad expanses of Lapland's open terrain, creatures as unrelated as the stoat, blue hare, arctic fox and ptarmigan share the same characteristic: they adjust their colours according to the season, to blend with the prevailing ground cover and gain a measure of protection from their enemies. In the case of the predators, there is an added benefit: they are concealed from their prey as well, and thus have more chance of taking their victims by surprise.

In summer the animals are brown or mottled and difficult to spot against the blossoming colours of the landscape around them. But as the snows of winter approach, the shortening days and falling temperatures trigger a change in the body chemistry of these creatures. They stop almost all production of melanin, the dark pigment that gives colour to individual fibres of hair or feather. As the melanin disappears from their pelts and plumage, the animals and birds gradually turn white until, like the stoat in the photograph at far right, they are almost impossible to pick out against a background of snow.

In addition to offering these creatures camouflage, the snowy winter coat performs another more subtle but no less vital function. As the melanin vanishes, microscopic air pockets form in the fibres of fur and feather. These pockets serve to trap body heat. Thick, loose layers of soft undercoat or down, covered by coarser guard layers, trap and hold still more heat. Safe and warm in their quarters in the snow, the animals can withstand night-time temperatures as low as —58° F.

This protective coloration guards not only against predators and cold but, paradoxically, against heat as well. During spring and autumn, snow and warm sunshine can combine to pose a hazard as severe in its way as that of predators. The ptarmigan, for example, must spend hours out under the open sky, scraping away at the shallow surface snow or searching the windblown ridges for seeds and plants to eat.

So effectively insulated is this bird—and all the other white-garbed creatures—that the rays of the sun could cause dangerous overheating. But this does not happen. The very colours that camouflage the creatures during the time of the winter snow also help to keep them from overheating by day: the white effectively reflects the sun's rays.

A stoat peers from its rocky hiding place (above), its summer pelt helping it to merge with the surroundings. By winter (right) the coat—now called ermine—has turned white, camouflaging the stoat as it searches among the snowdrifts for birds and such mammals as the hare on which it can feed.

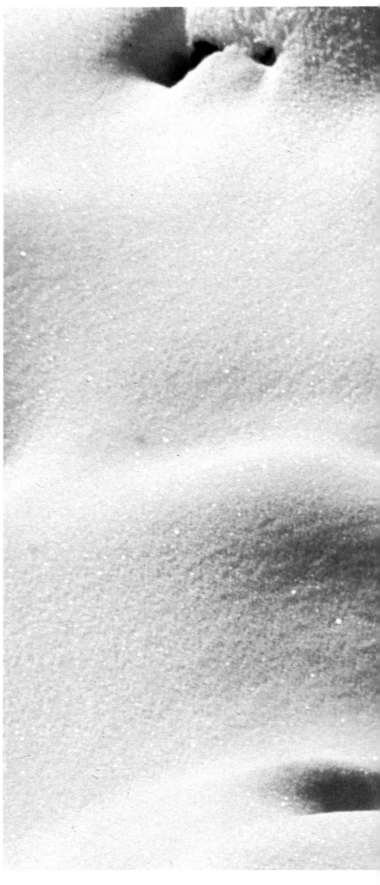

Its brown summer fur looking pale in the glare of the photographer's flashgun, a blue hare (above) forages among the Lapland vegetation. In spring and autumn the brown hairs of the summer coat mingle with the white of the winter coat, giving the animal a blue appearance and accounting for its name.

Clad in white winter coat (right) the hare pauses on the snow. But deep snow impedes its movements, so that even winter camouflage may not provide sufficient protection against persistent predators, including the arctic fox, which pick up a trail in the snow and follow it until their quarry is cornered.

In its sleek summer coat (above), an arctic fox prowls across Lapland's high stony ground. Its diet includes voles, hares and birds and their eggs. But its main food is lemming and the regular fluctuations in lemming populations are reflected in the numbers of foxes.

Looking almost cub-like in its fluffy, cold-proof winter coat (right), an adult arctic fox searches for the tracks of small animals or birds. When prey is really scarce, the fox can survive on the secret cache it has accumulated during the summer months of plenty.

The breeding plumage of the male ptarmigan (above) provides camouflage among the spring colours. One of the few birds to develop three distinct plumages to match the changes in the coloration of its habitat, the ptarmigan becomes predominantly grey in autumn and almost pure white in winter.

A male ptarmigan garbed in protective winter white (right) has a black line running round the eye that distinguishes it from the female in similar plumage. The black tail and flight feathers (not visible in this picture) of both sexes help to break up their outlines in flight and confuse aerial predators.

2/ In the Grip of the Glaciers

In the Lapland mountains . . . the atmosphere of the
wilderness [is] a tangible reality that cannot be
felt so truly and intensely anywhere else in Europe.

GOSTA LUNDQUIST AND OLOF THANING/ *LAPLAND*

The Lapland wilderness does not give up its secrets easily and travellers more familiar with the green lushness of temperate Europe may fail to be immediately impressed by the stark colouring of Lapland's landscape, the pale glare of the unsinking summer sun and its rich though often elusive wildlife. To such travellers the words of Francesco Negri, an Italian priest who visited Lapland in the middle of the 17th Century, may still seem depressingly accurate.

"The cold is of such rigour," wrote Negri, "that for eight months of the year snow and ice cover all land and all water. And these may in part remain two months more, so that only July and August are free from winter's grip. On the higher mountains lies an unchanging snow-cap, and to a depth of a foot or two feet beneath the ground, frost prevails. In many a marshy place, you may find ice throughout every season; while as for summer, the air is noxious with mosquitoes and midges which come in such hosts that the sun is obscured. All this being so, one would surely hold that the country cannot be inhabited by so much as wild beasts. It must surely be a desert."

Yet, Negri also called Lapland "the whole glorious book of nature". What he meant was that this deceptive land could be appreciated only by those with the skill to see past its superficial appearance. And as I wished to sharpen my own perceptions of the land I decided to travel to the mountains where the forces that helped to shape it are still active.

I set out early one morning by car for the high range of the Lyngen peninsula, a rugged finger of land to the east of Tromsø that points to the Arctic Ocean. Here glaciers grind remorseless paths from snow-capped summits, continuing the erosive work of the great ice sheet that once inundated Scandinavia and reached out to embrace a huge part of the Northern Hemisphere during the Ice Age.

The term "Ice Age" is misleading, for there have been many periods of extensive glaciation in the earth's history, the earliest dating back at least 600 million years. But the period generally known as the Ice Age, properly called the Pleistocene Epoch, commenced approximately two million years ago, at about the same time that the first man was emerging in Africa, and ended only 10,000 years ago.

During the intervening span at least four major advances of the ice, separated by milder phases, spread across northern Europe, Asia and America, leaving an indelible imprint on the land. Lapland, so far north, was one of the first regions to be enveloped by the ice, and one of the last to be freed from its life-destroying grip.

No one can account with certainty for the causes of the Ice Age. A short-term reduction in the output of solar radiation, a massive eruption of volcanic dust that obscured the sun, a slight variation in the earth's movement around the sun affecting the distribution of solar heat received at the earth's surface—all are possible causes of the drop in mean annual temperature that must immediately have preceded the formation of ice sheets. Whatever the cause, the temperature did drop; summers grew shorter and colder, winters longer and more intense. Gradually, first in arctic regions and then farther south, glaciers began to form in the mountains.

In Lapland, the glaciers advanced from the mountains, merging with others edging down from the Swedish uplands. The ice spread westwards, gouging out great valleys that are now Scandinavia's fjords. It spread eastwards, helping to mould the Lapland fells into smooth, elongated humps whose crests were swept parallel to the direction of the ice flow. Farther east, where they encountered softer rock formations, the glaciers scooped out depressions and hollows that, when the ice melted, became part of the countless lakes of Finnish Lapland.

Evidence of the glacial advance can be seen everywhere one looks in Lapland. To the south of Tromsø I passed a large boulder of red granite that was perched incongruously among the hills, far from any outcrop of similar rock. It was an erratic, a geological fragment that had been transported by the moving ice a distance of nearly one hundred

46/

miles from its pre-glacial position on the Norwegian-Swedish border.

Later on my travels, around the treeless, boulder-strewn peninsula of North Varanger, in north-east Lapland, I was to see just how dramatically the ice had sculpted the land. In that bleak region, where a scanty soil cover barely disguises the solid bedrock, glacial scars show up livid on hills, and exposed rock surfaces are fluted and grooved with parallel scratches that resemble the claw marks of a bear.

At the peak of the glacial advance, the ice mass completely covered Lapland, rising in a great dome-shaped sheet that must have been 10,000 feet thick at the centre and spread southwest towards the British Isles and south to northern Germany.

As more and more water became locked up as glacial ice, the oceans shrank until the sea-level was 300 feet lower than it is today. Paradoxically, this shrinkage did not increase the land area, for the sheer weight of the ice depressed the region as much as 3,000 feet into the earth's crust. Glaciated valleys were drowned and Scandinavia's coastline became a confusion of fjords, inlets, islands and peninsulas.

It is difficult to envisage a land sinking into the earth's crust, and just as difficult to envisage it rising again. Yet this has happened—and is still happening in parts of Lapland. As the ice sheets waned, the land, freed from its glacial burden, began to recoil from its entrenched position. The process has been slow and uneven, and wave action on the exposed coastline has cut successive marine terraces that are so clearly defined that they look like tramlines. Parts of Lapland are still rising, although at the much reduced rate of about one centimetre a year.

Long before the ice mass had reduced Lapland to a glacial desert, those plants and animals that were able to do so moved southwards to regions where falling temperatures had created environments similar to those they were being forced to abandon. Members of species that could not move before the advancing ice—mainly annual plants and sedentary insects—died, except perhaps in areas that may have remained ice-free throughout the glacial period. A few of these refuges, called nunataks, almost certainly existed in Lapland, for although the ice sheet was 10,000 feet thick at its centre, it was thinner in the western mountains, and individual peaks jutted above its surface. In these refuges, hardy plants, such as lichens and mosses, would have fought for a precarious existence, in turn providing food for a few insects and possibly such mammals and birds as the lemming and the ptarmigan.

Driving from Tromsø in the warm sun along a road that skirted the glittering blue waters of Balsfjord I found it hard to realize that these

The North Cape, the legendary northernmost point of Lapland—and of western Europe—plunges through mist into the placid waters of the Arctic Ocean. Some experts believe that, until 10,000 years ago, these headlands were blanketed by a vast ice-sheet that stretched far out to sea. When the ice melted, the rising water level filled the glacier-gouged bays and fjords.

isolated communities of plants and animals would once have been the only living things in an otherwise frozen and silent landscape. The road turned abruptly at right angles and plunged for about 15 miles through a jumble of mountains that rose to more than 5,000 feet. Ahead I caught a glimpse of the sea, and minutes later I arrived at the tiny hamlet of Breivikedeit, on the shores of Ullsfjord. Here I waited for the ferry that would take me across the two miles of water separating this part of Lapland from the Lyngen peninsula.

Lyngen filled the horizon to the east, a series of grim rock walls sweeping up to ice-capped peaks. Halfway down the western flank of the peninsula, and at the end of a narrow fjord that nips the mountain range into two, is the village of Lyngseidet. It was near here that I pitched camp in the late evening. Jiekkevarre, a 6,000-foot summit that straddles the southern half of the peninsula, and is referred to by mountaineers as the Mont Blanc of the North, lies some 15 miles south-west of the village. This mountain was to be my target the following day.

Although the journey from Tromsø had tired me, I lay restlessly in my sleeping-bag, unable to turn my thoughts away from the glacial desert that had once covered Lapland. It was about 12,000 years ago—a mere fraction of time in the area's history—that the climate began to change. For reasons as hard to fathom as those that had caused the onset of the Ice Age, it grew milder, the warming influence of the Gulf Stream asserted itself, and Lapland's ice-sheet began to melt.

Grudgingly, it withdrew first from the warmer west coast and then, slowly and spasmodically, from the east and the south, creating distinctive landforms on the newly-bared and rocky surface. Large, crescent-shaped ridges, known as recessional moraines, were formed from débris deposited by the retreating ice, and egg-shaped hillocks, called drumlins, which had been built up during the glacial advance, were uncovered. Boulder clay—an unsorted mixture of rocks, gravel, sand and clay—collected on the plains and in the valleys, providing the basis of a life-supporting soil.

Lapland was a region reborn. For in the wake of the ice came those species that were able to colonize glacial soils leached of almost all organic nutrients. First of these colonizers were the lichens, mosses and algae, and as they died and rotted, they enriched the soil with their remains, establishing conditions for species with more specialized growing requirements.

Pollen analyses of different soil layers in Finnish Lapland have provided a vivid record of this post-glacial succession, revealing that a vegetation made up of creeping herbs and grasses soon established itself over much of the region and that this was followed by birches and willows invading from the south. These trees are rapid growers, with high reproductive capacities and effective seed dispersal mechanisms, and they quickly reclaimed all but the harshest habitats.

But their supremacy lasted only some 2,000 years. Slower growing pines gradually encroached until, 6,000 years ago, they had become what ecologists call a climax vegetation. In other words, they formed a more or less stable and self-perpetuating community. Pine is still the predominant climax vegetation over much of Lapland, but for the last 3,000 years spruce, invading from the great taiga in the east, has made inroads in the pine forests, establishing itself on the western flank of the Scandinavian mountain chain.

The post-glacial succession in Lapland did not progress smoothly and uniformly. At times a return to colder conditions brought about a renewal of glacial activity (terminal moraines far in front of the snouts of Lapland's present-day glaciers indicate the extent of these earlier advances by the ice) and an overall slowing down of the succession. At other times, the temperature rose above today's levels and there was a vigorous upsurge of life. There is evidence that about 5,000 years ago Lapland went through its warmest period—the "climatic optimum"—with a mean annual temperature of around 40°F., some 5°F. higher than at present. Fossil remains dating from this period show that the upper limit of pines was then 600 feet higher than it is today.

To complicate the pattern of post-glacial succession further, not all species invaded Lapland along a single front. At the same time as alpine plants were recolonizing Lapland from the south, it is probable that similar species that had survived the Ice Age on nunataks began to spread out from their mountain refuges. However, so rapidly did the forests establish themselves on the lowlands that they would effectively have formed a barrier preventing the two colonizing groups from linking up. Many alpine plants did eventually penetrate the less densely forested borders of Lapland to the north and the east, but some species, such as the slender gentian and alpine butterwort, never succeeded in forming a single, unbroken distribution range through the area.

The fauna that returned to Lapland in the wake of the last great glaciation had changed little during its time farther south. There were some casualties, particularly among the larger mammals: the mammoth and the woolly rhinoceros became extinct in the immediate post-glacial

Smooth-worn mountainsides and a stark terrain show the abrasive effects of the glacial ice.

Rugged Landscapes Shaped by Ice

More than 10,000 years after the last great Ice Age, the relief of Lapland remains a visual record of the impact it had on the region. In parts the ice lay almost two miles thick. In its slow, grinding movement, it wore down the bedrock, scoured out basin-like cirques from the head-walls of valleys, eroded and widened valley floors and swept away most of the surface soil. Then, as the climate grew warmer, the ice retreated across Lapland, dumping débris that formed the basis for fresh soil and encouraged colonization by hardy plants.

Even today the land is responding to the effects of Ice Age glaciation: the ground, so long depressed by the enormous weight of the thick ice-sheet, is slowly rising again.

Surrounded by ice-gouged lakes, the winding ridges crossing the bog were formed from sediment carried by streams that ran in or under the ice.

Bounded by soaring slopes, a lake in Sarek National Park, Sweden, lies in a deep valley carved by a glacier.

period, possibly as a result of man's uncontrolled hunting, but the reindeer, lemming, arctic fox, brown bear, wolf and wolverine all survived to re-establish themselves as a distinctive part of Lapland's fauna.

Birds also returned, but because most of them are active in daylight and are unable to find sufficient food on thickly snow-covered ground, only a few have been able to adapt themselves to Lapland's dark and bitter winters and so the majority are seasonal visitors.

My preoccupation with the events that had shaped Lapland and the fact that the summer sun did not sink while I tried to sleep made me so restless that I decided to rise and make an early start for Jiekkevarre. From Lyngenfjord the valley of Lyngsdalen funnels westwards up to Jiekkevarre. Since my map indicated no major obstacles along the course of the valley, I reckoned that nothing more than a hard slog would take me up at least as far as the snow-line. The road on which I drove to Lyngsdalen is bounded on one side by Lyngenfjord and on the other by a range of towering mountains from which avalanches of snow and rock can come crashing down during the spring thaw. This, of course, was summer, but I cannot say that I was very sorry to leave the road, park my car and begin my trek up the Lyngsdalen valley.

I had not gone far when I encountered an unexpected difficulty: my path was blocked by a tangled mass of vegetation which, as I approached, became recognizable as dense thickets of alders and willows growing so closely together that they formed a kind of arctic jungle. The ground gradually became waterlogged until I found myself in the middle of a bog, a quaking fen where ferns and mosses disguised stinking black pools of stagnant water. There seemed to be no way round this morass, so treading warily, I edged farther in, choosing a route where the vegetation seemed to offer the easiest passage.

It was warm in the shade of the alders and, when I stopped my squelching progress, eerily silent. The trees, deprived of a compact soil to bind their roots and give stability to their trunks, grew at crazy angles or sprawled along the ground, where half-submerged roots and branches kept snaring my stumbling feet. Round the bases of the alders there were tall clusters of slender wands that whipped back to sting my legs as I pushed through them.

After some minutes of toiling through this morass, I was sweating quite heavily and had been reduced to such frenzied exasperation that when yet another branch barred my way, I pulled out my knife, hacked at it and wrenched it off. Shockingly, the wounded stem began to bleed.

It was no use telling myself that the bright orange liquid that slowly welled from the gash was merely sap; to me it resembled blood.

After this unnerving experience, my one thought was to get clear of the trees and on to open ground. Yet, irritated as I was by my slow and painful progress, I was also curious to find out how soil so waterlogged could support such dense growth. To survive, trees need nitrogen; they are unable to absorb this directly from the air, but their needs are met by soil bacteria. These convert atmospheric nitrogen into soluble nitrates that the trees absorb through their roots. Flooded soils, however, are devoid of the oxygen that the bacteria require. How, then, did these alders, which, in spite of their marshy habitat, were perfectly healthy, obtain their life-giving nitrogen?

Small, wart-like nodules that I found on many of the alder roots provided the answer. Inside these were the nitrogen-fixing bacteria, synthesizing nitrates from the air and, in return, being supplied with oxygen by the trees. The association is an important one, since it allows the alders to colonize where other trees are unable to survive. In time the alders, by a process of death, decay and regeneration, would produce a deeper, more fertile soil and raise the land above water level. Other trees, such as birch and pine, would then gradually move in and oust the alders. In 50 years, perhaps less, it would be difficult to imagine that this tangled marsh had existed.

At last I struggled clear of the alders and came out on to the fells— treeless, windy slopes tilted at a daunting angle towards Jiekkevarre's bare shoulder. I paused to rest, by the skeleton of a reindeer that had broken its leg and died here. A hare, disturbed by my approach, scuttled for shelter among slabs of rock that were covered with dark mosses and bright orange lichens. In a depression near by, an old fall of snow fringed a small pool where shelves of ice showed startlingly blue beneath the surface. As I watched, a brittle, floating husk of ice drifted before the light wind and against the shore.

I was startled by a sound behind me, like two pebbles being clicked together. Looking round, I could see nothing at first, but the sound persisted and eventually a flicker of movement betrayed a cock wheatear perched on a rock. I stayed very still, not wishing to frighten the bird, and for several more minutes it remained on the rock making its tuneless, clicking call. Then suddenly it flew off beyond the brow of the hill. It was an early hour for birds to be active, but probably the wheatear had a nest of newly-hatched young hidden in some near-by crevice, and was taking full advantage of the 24 hours of daylight to get them fully fledged before the short Lapland summer drew to a close.

As I came nearer to Jiekkevarre, the ascent grew even steeper and I had to concentrate on the ground immediately ahead of me. But I paused from time to time to scan the landscape for other birds. The golden eagle still nests in isolated valleys in spite of harassment by herders who claim that it takes their spring reindeer-calves. In fact, mountain hares and ptarmigan form the bulk of the eagle's living prey, and in winter it is often forced to forsake its regal image and subsist on carrion such as the dead reindeer whose skeleton I had seen earlier.

A hunting eagle is one of the most dramatic sights that Lapland can provide. Often, the first indication that this feathered killer is in the vicinity is a flurry of movement from some high slope as a panic-stricken covey of ptarmigan spy their enemy. Seconds later, the eagle appears over the skyline, deceptively slow in flight, but gaining on the weakest member of the covey with the speed of an express train. The victim is squeezed to death in the eagle's vicious talons and is usually carried off to a convenient mound to be eaten. If the victim is too heavy, its killer will bear it to the ground and begin the meal immediately.

If the golden eagle represents power and majesty, that other raptor of the mountains, the gyr falcon, is the epitome of speed and manoeuvrability. It is larger than the peregrine, which in Lapland is approaching the northern limits of its range, and has lighter plumage and heavier wings. The gyr falcon flies low and fast over the hillside, following the contours, hoping to startle a ptarmigan into flight and clutch it with a sudden burst of acceleration. Occasionally, it indulges in a more spectacular display. Perched immobile on some crag, it waits for a victim to fly beneath it. Then it launches itself, rolls over and descends in a vertical power dive. Usually the prey is killed by a blow from the falcon's talons and is picked up in mid-air and carried to a mound to be eaten. But if the prey is crippled and falls to the ground, the falcon descends in spirals and breaks the victim's neck with its strong, notched beak.

The gyr falcon's hunting prowess did not escape the attention of the medieval falconers, who prized it above all other falcons. In the 13th-Century English treatise, *The Boke of St. Albans*, the author allocated the "eagle for an emperor", the "gyr falcon for a king", while a mere earl had to make do with a peregrine. Always searching for the perfect hunter, falconers were among the first travellers to Lapland, where they collected the young falcons for sale to the courts of Europe. How valuable they were can be deduced from the fact that a Crusader captured by the Saracens had to supply a pair of gyr falcons as a ransom.

Lapland miniatures

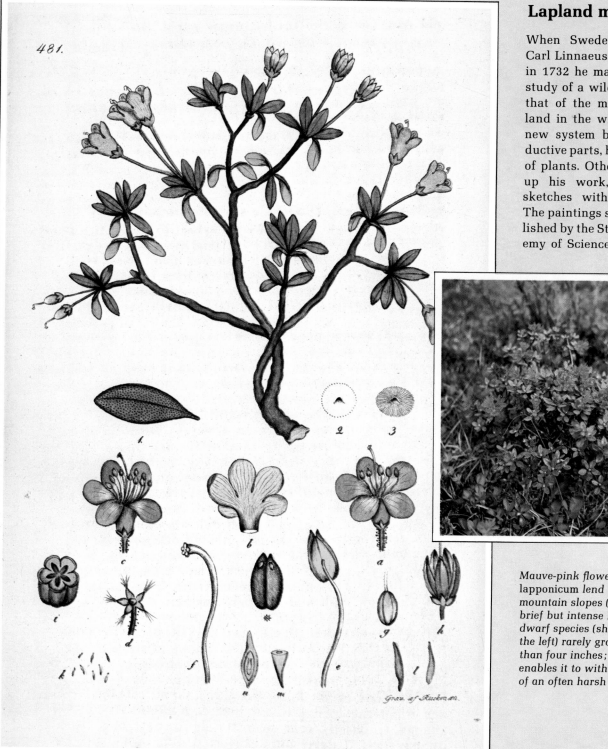

481.

When Sweden's great naturalist, Carl Linnaeus, travelled to Lapland in 1732 he made the first scientific study of a wildlife "as unknown as that of the most barbaric tract of land in the whole world". Using a new system based on their reproductive parts, he classified hundreds of plants. Other scientists followed up his work, supplementing his sketches with detailed paintings. The paintings shown here were published by the Stockholm Royal Academy of Sciences in the early 1800s.

Mauve-pink flowers of Rhododendron lapponicum lend their vivid colour to mountain slopes (above) early in the brief but intense Lapland summer. This dwarf species (shown in the painting on the left) rarely grows to a height of more than four inches; but its stunted growth enables it to withstand the biting winds of an often harsh environment.

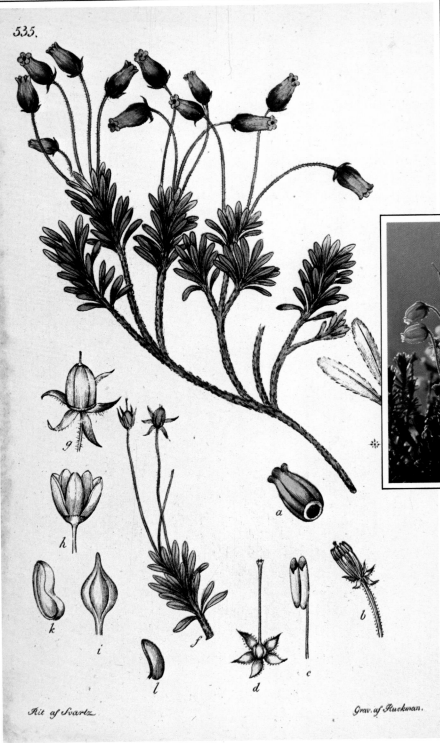

Resembling miniature flasks in the painting (left), the slender-stalked flowers of Phyllodoce caerulea (above) carpet alpine and lowland heath. They are pollinated by bees and other long-tongued insects able to reach into their elongated blooms for nectar. The evergreen leaves that clothe the lower parts are resistant to extreme cold.

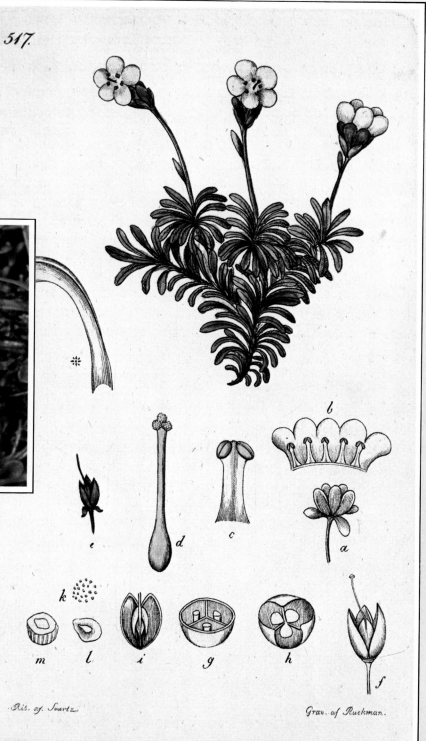

517.

Ril. of Svartz.   Grav. of Ruckman.

Rosettes of leaves on the evergreen
Diapensia lapponica (painted at right)
become so densely tangled that they
form a springy, cushionlike mass up
to about two inches thick. The only
representative of its family growing
wild on the continent of Europe, the
plant can be found on stony ground
and in the crevices of rocks.

Watching for gyr falcons, I recalled an occasion on the fells of Swedish Lapland when I had found a dead lemming, its skull crushed and a large wound in its belly. As I examined it, I was suddenly aware that I was not alone, a disquieting sensation in such wild country. I looked about, but nothing stirred, then, glancing upwards, I saw three large, white-bellied birds, hawklike and with long, forked tails, skimming the hillside with effortless ease. They were long-tailed skuas, the pirates of the fells, which live by harrying other birds and forcing them to disgorge their prey. At times, they kill their own quarry, and when lemmings have a peak year they feed largely on these creatures, breeding in scattered colonies where the rodent population is densest. So long as I was in evidence, they kept their distance from the dead lemming.

Although I continued to keep a sharp lookout on my approach to Jiekkevarre, the wheatear was the only bird I saw. But there were compensations. In the more sheltered places I passed expanses of white arctic bell heather, stands of Lapland rhododendron and clumps of bilberry and cotton grass. In one secluded spot I stopped to photograph a carpet of alpine flowers whose colours glowed with an almost luminous intensity compared with lowland plants. There were pink crowberry flowers dominating the purple, flask-shaped blooms of mountain heath; while Lapland *Diapensia* clustered in dense rosettes, their old leaves playing host to a tiny lichen that is found on no other plant. Elsewhere, bearberry formed a creeping mat, some of its leaves already stained red, as though autumn had arrived early.

I lingered here awhile. The fells, I knew, are not always so inviting. In spring, when floods of meltwater come streaming off the mountains, transforming the hulking forelands into sleekly shining obstacle courses, they can be hell to walk over. During this season the melting snow and ice deluge the land, turning brooks into torrents, flooding valley bottoms and drowning animals in their burrows. For a week or two it is difficult to move about. But such conditions are worth enduring, for once you hear the ice breaking up on the rivers, you know that the long winter is over and that soon the seemingly dead land will again be bursting into new life.

As soon as the fells are free of snow, they become the breeding grounds of many birds newly arrived from their winter quarters in the lowlands and the south. Territories are chosen, proclaimed by song and defended against rivals. Females are courted, again by song and by often elaborate display flights.

This is the best time to watch the dotterel which, with its white eye-stripe, chestnut breast and black belly, is one of the handsomest of mountain birds. It is also remarkably tame; I have observed the female close at hand, scraping in several places before deciding where to lay her eggs. After laying, the hen leaves the incubation to the cock because only he has brood patches, those areas of bare skin rich in blood vessels that conduct body heat directly to the eggs. A certain absentmindedness in affairs of the heart seems to characterize the hen. Sometimes she forgets that she has already accepted a mate and succumbs to the blandishments of a second.

No such infidelity occurs with those other birds of the high slopes, the ptarmigan. They are monogamous, pairing for life, and the cock guards the sitting hen with a devotion amounting to bravado. Throughout the incubation period, he stands on a rock or hummock near the nest and protests noisily, with tail raised and wings drooping, if a predator should venture too close.

As I left the fells and began struggling up through the zone of bare rock that leads to Jiekkevarre's snow-line, I heard the brief, piping song of the snow bunting, a sweetly soulful sound in such desolate surroundings. But although I paused frequently during my climb up the rock slope, the only other sound I heard was that of a black-throated diver echoing from a lake far below. Its faint, haunting cry increased my sense of melancholy isolation, for I seemed to have reached a point where life had given up its struggle against the intractable elements.

Yet this was only an illusion. Life does exist at this altitude, but it exists in miniature, in isolated places hidden from the wind and snow. Lichens grew here, forming flat yellow, grey and brown crusts that seemed to be integral parts of the rock to which they clung. To me they appeared more mineral than vegetable, although I knew that not only are they living organisms, but that each lichen is a complex structure made up of two plant species, a fungus and an alga.

The association is a symbiotic one, in which each partner is dependent on the other. It seems that, as the fungus lacks the chlorophyll necessary for the photosynthesis of organic nutrients, these are supplied by the alga. In return for this, the alga, which demands a moist environment, is supplied with water by the highly absorbent fungus and may also receive essential mineral salts that the fungus has derived from the rock on which it grows.

Up here, the lichens are pioneer plants—just as the alders are below—and they literally break new ground. They may live for hundreds of years, coalescing and extending in size until a single area of lichen growth may be up to five feet square. During all this time the fungal partner secretes organic acids that slowly dissolve the underlying rock in an immeasurably slow process of chemical erosion. Combined with rotting particles of old lichen growth, tiny rock fragments are displaced and slither to the ground where, trapped in cracks and crevices, they form the basis of a soil in which other plants can grow.

Higher still, even the tenacious lichens often cannot survive. For some time, as I picked my way through the tumbled rocks and detritus, I had been skirting isolated patches of snow which, as I climbed and the air grew colder, merged into an unbroken mantle of white. I had reached the snow-line. Venturing on to this blanket, I was surprised to see that the snow beneath my boots turned red wherever I trod. It was not until much later that I discovered the cause. Vast numbers of green algae grow in polar snows and high on mountains. As aquatic plants, they build up food reserves from elements in the snow itself. Their chlorophyll is masked by a red pigment called haematochrome, which protects them from extreme cold and intense sunlight. It was this pigment that had caused the staining.

I continued to climb for a while, but the snow and the mountain's ever-increasing steepness were not to be overcome. Before turning back, however, I rested and gazed at the landscape. Far below I could see where forested slopes, slashed by ravines, gave way to the fells I had so painfully traversed. Some had stony tracts that made my feet ache to look at them. Others rose in steep, smoothed humps. To the north, jagged peaks project into the sky; southwards, the summits gradually decrease in size until they are lost in the distance and join the main link of the Scandinavian mountain chain stretching more than one thousand miles to the south of Norway.

Glancing from summit to summit, I recalled that they are nearly all about the same height. It did not require much imagination to see that if the intervening valleys were filled to the level of the peaks, the land would form an uplifted and almost level plateau. Such a plateau did once exist, but over the thousands of centuries it has been carved into its present deeply dissected form.

The process is far from over. Each year rain and meltwater flooding down the slopes deepens valleys and carries away more and more rock; wind smoothes exposed surfaces; frost shatters cliff faces, sending fragments tumbling down to form layers of scree below. Water trapped in cracks and crevices freezes at night and expands with a force that can fracture boulders. Even the tiny lichens play their part in a dynamic process that will not end until the mountains themselves have been washed down to the sea.

Of all these erosive forces, ice is still the most potent. Some experts believe that Lapland's present-day glaciers are remnants of the last glacial advance, others that they formed much later. Whatever the truth, the ice is continuing a process that began two million years ago. From my vantage point I could see where tongues of snow-covered ice had licked down from Jiekkevarre's summit through valleys gouged out by previous glaciations. Aided by the abrasive power of dust, stones and boulders scraped from valley walls, the ice is continually scarring and scooping away at the bedrock.

By Ice Age standards, of course, today's glaciers are minute and they are steadily growing smaller. After 1920 Lapland entered a warm phase and since that date most glaciers have been retreating farther up the mountains, the birch and pine forests have extended their range northwards, and with them have come forest-loving animals such as the lynx and the roe deer.

Yet, as I made my way back down Jiekkevarre's slopes, I wondered how long this regeneration of life would continue. Ever since the turn of the century, when geologists first established that the Ice Age was not simply a period of sustained and lasting cold, but a succession of cold and warm phases, it has been argued that the Ice Age has not ended, that we are living in an interglacial period, and that some day a rapidly cooling climate will precipitate another glacial advance.

Certainly, up here in the Lapland mountains, where time has still not obliterated the ravages of the frozen past, it is impossible to escape the feeling that the last 10,000 years have been no more than a respite. The glaciers on Jiekkevarre are small now, and becoming smaller. But one day, perhaps sooner than anyone anticipates, they may grow again, spread out from the mountains and turn Lapland once more into a frigid, white desert.

The Tenacious Lichens

In those parts of Lapland that are most exposed to winter's merciless assault, the plants with the best chance of survival are the lichens. Clinging to rocks and trees, they defy, snow, ice and desiccating winds. Lichens are no ordinary plants. Each species consists, in fact, of two plants—a fungus and an alga—which co-exist in a mutually beneficial partnership and develop as a single structure.

Because of their dual nature, lichens grow in a complex manner, and their intricate shapes have a frail beauty, which is shown by the examples on the following pages. In spite of their apparent fragility, however, each is perfectly adapted to the rigours of arctic living. The spongy fungal partner weaves a web of tough threads round the alga, shielding it from the elements and helping to supply it with water. In return, the alga photosynthesizes the organic nutrients that both partners share. Photosynthesis continues even when the temperature plummets to —11° F., and the lichens can withstand still more intense cold, or periods of drought, by going into a state of suspended animation.

Lichens have two main methods of reproduction. The fungal partner in many species produces spores that must link up with an appropriate alga to form a new plant. Other lichens reproduce vegetatively; fragments of the mature plant break off and may lodge in a suitable environment where they continue to grow. Some species resort to a refinement of this method by releasing strands of fungal and algal cells that develop eventually into self-sufficient plants.

Once the vital partnership between fungus and alga is established, the lichen grows slowly but inexorably. Although five millimetres a year is a rapid growth-rate for rock-bound species, their tenacity is so great that they can live for centuries, making them among the world's oldest living things. Their great longevity has benefits for geologists who, by calculating the age of the oldest lichen on a glacial moraine can gauge when the débris was laid down and thus plot a particular glacier's movements.

For all their resilience, lichens have one fatal weakness: most are highly vulnerable to air pollution. Even in Lapland's pure air many species have been contaminated by radioactive fallout from nuclear tests thousands of miles away.

Frond-like growths on Hypogymnia physodes give this lichen a convoluted and brain-like texture. Each outgrowth is potentially a young lichen. During summer the outgrowths dry up, become brittle and are readily dislodged, to be borne away by the wind to some crevice where, under the right conditions, they grow into replicas of the adult plant.

64/

Dark red patches on the surface of
Haematomma ventosum (above) are
fungal reproductive organs, each
producing eight spores. The yellowish
colour of the main body is caused by
usnic acid, an antibiotic substance that
inhibits the growth of harmful bacteria.

Slow-growing crusts of Rhizocarpon
geographicum (right) form a mosaic on
a rock. This very long-lived lichen is
common on glacial moraines and it is
used by geologists for the technique
called lichenometry—the use of lichens
for gauging the age of rock surfaces.

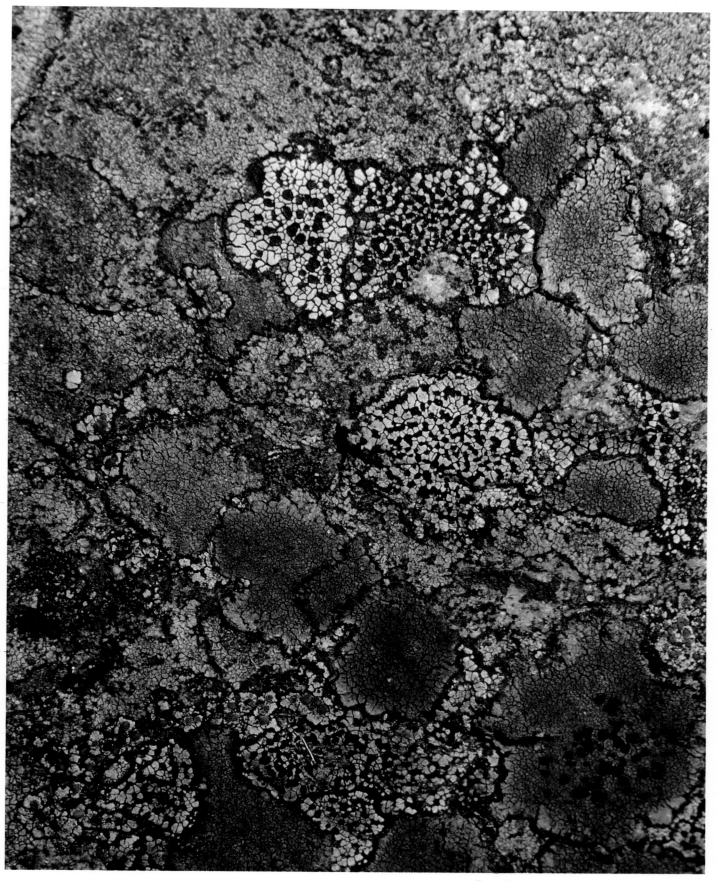

Wrinkled and ridged like a coral,
Parmelia sulcata *looks more mineral*
than vegetable. The powdery granules
scattered over its surface are loose
aggregates of fungal and algal cells,
called soredia, that are capable of
reproducing the lichen vegetatively.

The bright yellow-lobed lichen
Xanthoria parientina was believed in
the Middle Ages to be an effective cure
for jaundice. The medieval belief was
that God had marked plants suitable
for treating diseases by making them
resemble the afflicted parts of the body.

A tangled mat of threads give Ramalina polymorpha a large surface area, allowing the lichen to absorb many times its own weight of water directly from the air. But it pays a penalty for this. Pollutants are also absorbed, and when they reach a critical level the lichen degenerates and dies.

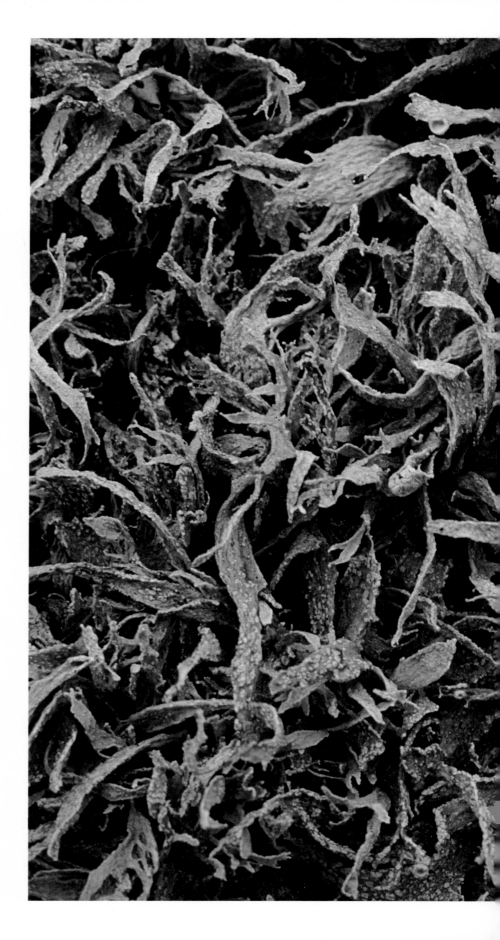

3/ The Heartland

It was afternoon before I reached Alta and, leaving the Norwegian Sea behind me, turned south, heading into the heart of the Lapland plateau. I had left the Lyngen peninsula early that morning and the mountains were now lost over the horizon to the west, 80 miles away on the map, but three times that distance by the twisting coastal road I had followed round the north-west corner of Lapland.

My destination was Kautokeino, the most important of the Lapp settlements, a mustering place on the reindeer-herders' route between their summer pastures on the coast and their winter quarters in the interior. For many of the nomads it is a kind of spiritual home, a place where weddings, births and funerals take place and where, at Easter, reindeer races are held along the frozen course of the river Alta. For me Kautokeino had another attraction.

Roughly equidistant from the mountains in the west, the arctic seas in the north and the Russian forests in the east, the settlement lies at the heart of the Lapland plateau, a 200-square-mile tract of fells, bogs, lakes and rivers that is regarded by many to be the most distinctive part of the Lapland wilderness. Certainly, there are few other places, even in this wild country, that give an appearance of such total desolation. South of the tremendous gorge sliced by the river Alta on its way to the sea, I pulled over to the side of the road and got out of the car to stretch my legs. With the engine switched off, the silence was absolute: not a bird called, not a leaf rustled. I felt the same overwhelming sense of isolation that I had experienced during my climb above the snow-line on Jiekkevarre. Behind and ahead of me the road stretched away, apparently going nowhere. On each side of it the ridges spread in endless succession. There were no jagged peaks here to lend distance and perspective to the landscape, no snowfields or forests to relieve the camouflage vista of brown and grey.

The Norwegians call this plateau the *vidda*, a word that defies exact translation, but which signifies a wild, open place, rather like the English word "moor". The word is sometimes translated as "desert", and it is true that at first glance this generally treeless waste seems incapable of supporting life. In another sense, the word "desert" is apt, for the vidda lies in the rain-shadow cast by the Lapland mountains, and although clouds hang above the fells for most of the year, precipitation amounts to no more than 12 inches a year—less than received by Alice Springs in the middle of the Australian Outback.

But here the comparison with the desert ends. The mountains that shield the vidda from the rain also sap the winds blowing off the Atlantic Ocean of their warmth. Winter on the plateau is long and harsh, with temperatures often plunging below $-36°F$, so that what moisture the winds carry during this period falls as snow. All through the winter months the snow and ice accumulates, forming a reservoir of water that sustains plant growth during the comparatively hot, dry summers.

Bogs chequer the plateau and it is these, together with the comparative absence of trees, that give the landscape its barren, tundra-like appearance. But again, the similarity is superficial. True tundra is characterized by a subsoil that is permanently frozen from a depth of about two feet to more than a hundred feet. Trees cannot grow on tundra because summer temperatures are too low for the germination and growth of tree seeds; and bogs are common in tundra regions because summer meltwater cannot percolate through the permafrost, and is trapped in shallow, stagnant ponds on the surface.

But only a tiny part of Lapland has such conditions and on the vidda completely different processes have been at work. The dearth of trees is due to the strong winds that sweep across the upland plateau, and in sheltered hollows stands of straggling birches do occur. The prevalence of bogs is a legacy of the Ice Age, when glaciers dumped their loads of eroded material on the plateau—creating a poor drainage system. In fact, the vidda is so poorly drained that when the spring thaw melts the snow-cover, much of the region becomes waterlogged. Later I was to see how some of the plants have adapted themselves to this environment.

The spring thaw on the plateau not only brings an upsurge of plant growth, it also signals a massive invasion. Birds, mostly waders and waterfowl, wing their way north from their winter quarters to breed, joining the handful of species, such as the ptarmigan and the snowy owl, that have braved the long winter on the vidda. I had arrived in Lapland too late to see this invasion and the hectic weeks of courtship, mating and breeding that follow it, but many species were still tending their young, some were laying a second clutch of eggs, and it would be several weeks before the mass exodus south began.

Now, however, nothing was stirring. Perhaps it was too hot: for the last few days the midday temperature had averaged 85° F. In vain I scanned the area for some sign of life and was just about to return to the car and drive on when I noticed a strange-looking mound on the slope of a near-by fell. What first caught my eye was the bright splash of green that surrounded the mound and was in marked contrast to the subdued tones of the prevailing vegetation. Curious to know what had caused this phenomenon, I left the road to investigate.

Drawing closer, I saw that the mound was about three feet high and hollowed out so that it resembled a miniature volcano. At first I thought it might be the abandoned lair of an arctic fox, but when I reached it I realized it was the old nesting site of a pair of snowy owls. This species does not build nests, but lays its eggs in depressions on high ground. Returning to the same nesting site year after year, the birds litter it with their droppings, which become mixed with the bones and feathers of small animals and birds, and pellets of regurgitated animal remains. It was accumulated débris of this kind that formed the mound and fertilized the surrounding soil, encouraging a richer, greener vegetation.

Although the nest was now deserted, it brought back vivid memories of a previous visit to the vidda when I had been involved in a sudden and dramatic confrontation with a pair of nesting snowy owls. It had occurred in early summer, on a day when a harsh wind blew curtains of rain and sleet across the fells. By late afternoon the rain stopped and the wind abated. But although my clothes were beginning to dry out all I could think of was the remote possibility of a hot bath. It was in this mood that, breasting the crest of a fell, I came almost face to face with a rather irate snowy owl.

The bird, a female, was squatting on a rock about 20 yards ahead. Far from being frightened by my approach, she seemed positively aggressive. Her snow-white feathers, heavily barred with black, were

Ponds formed by accumulated meltwater from snow and ice cover the vidda, the poorly-drained, desolate plateau of Norwegian Lapland.

ominously puffed up, and she had half spread her wings so as to look bigger. Her eyes, lemon-yellow, the pupils reduced to baleful slits, glared at me, and as I came closer she characteristically clacked her beak and let forth a sibilant hiss. Her mate, recognizable from the almost total lack of black markings on his plumage, flew up from a near-by knoll and silently, like some pale spectre, flapped in circles around my head.

I must have got to within ten feet of the female before she launched herself off the rock with a barking cry and swept past within inches of my head. I soon confirmed the reason for her defiance, for behind the rock was a nest-scrape containing five half-grown young, troll-like creatures swathed in sooty grey feathers. They rolled on to their backs when they saw me, and presented their clumsy but already formidable talons. I wanted to stay and photograph the nest, but a sudden rush of air above my head was enough to warn me that the female was trying to prevent my intrusion. Looking up I saw her banking round to make a second swoop, while her mate lurked menacingly a short distance away. I doubted that the female would press home her aerial assault, but I recalled that the eminent bird-photographer, Eric Hosking, had lost an eye to a nesting tawny owl, a species much smaller than the bird now diving towards me, so I decided to make a strategic withdrawal.

Significantly, that encounter had taken place in a lemming year, when a population explosion of the rodents had provided abundant feeding for predators. Snowy owls, which live almost exclusively on lemmings during the summer, had bred prolifically and laid unusually large clutches. Up to 13 eggs, double the usual number, were reported from a single nest, although not all the young survived to maturity. That is not surprising when you consider that a snowy owl fledgling may eat four lemmings a day. So in order to feed a nest of 13 the parent birds must catch about 50 lemmings every day before they can even think of feeding themselves. Inevitably, this quota was not met; some of the younger and weaker birds were deprived of prey by their elders, and were eventually killed and eaten by them.

My latest visit, however, was during a year when lemmings were scarce and the snowy owl population was forced to seek alternative prey, such as ptarmigan, mountain hares and waders. They had bred in low numbers, some adult pairs not breeding at all, thus compensating for the surplus population raised in former years. And this explained why the nest I had discovered was deserted.

Before resuming my journey to Kautokeino I decided to wander a little farther, and after descending the fell I made good progress over a carpet of reindeer moss. It had dried up in the summer heat and it crackled slightly beneath my feet. In summer the moss forms a thin skin, barely disguising the solid bedrock below. After walking for about 20 minutes I came across a scattering of stones arranged as if in a miniature Druid circle. Such circles are so regular that they are sometimes assumed to be man-made. They are, however, entirely natural phenomena characteristic of tundra and semi-tundra regions. Parts of the vidda, including the higher terrain around Masi, experience such severe winters that water trapped in the soil expands as it freezes and pushes a small area of soil upwards in a shallow dome that may measure ten feet across. Stones trapped in the dome act as "cold conductors": ice forms under them more rapidly than it does elsewhere and as this builds up the stones are pushed to the surface. The stones, under the influence of gravity, then gradually work their way down the icy dome and collect in a ring on the periphery.

Mud polygons, another variety of patterned ground, form when a severe drop in temperature from summer to winter causes areas of surface soil to contract. Around these areas, which may be 30 feet across, cracks develop in a striking polygonal pattern, and year after year the cracks become wider and deeper as snow and ice prise them apart. Another typical tundra phenomenon, that of soil flow or solifluction, occurs throughout the spring and summer, when rising temperatures thaw the icy surface soil causing it to flow slowly over the still-frozen ground beneath. The sludge, carrying a surface layer of vegetation with it, creeps downhill (even on slopes of no more than two or three degrees) and eventually accumulates at the foot of the slope. As spring succeeds spring, the effect of this process is to fill in depressions and, in a small way, flatten out Lapland's contours.

All these processes operate only on permanently waterlogged land that is subject to alternate freezing and thawing, and the Lapland plateau certainly has an abundance of that. Not far from the stone circle, my progress was barred by a line of bogs. No one who visits the vidda can travel far without encountering bogs, and to most people they are simply one of the less pleasant but inescapable features of the arctic, on a par with mosquitoes. Few bother to study them closely, and this is a pity, since they form an incredibly diverse environment that supports a host of highly specialized species.

More than 16 types of bog, classified according to the dominant vegetation that grows in them, have been identified in Lapland. But as I skirted the sodden ground I thought that this was probably too conservative an estimate. Some I saw were no more than shallow pools of stagnant water covered with a dirty layer of pollen and peat dust. They reminded me of the ponds of water pumped out from coal mines in industrial England. Others, on drier ground, were carpeted with a spongy mantle of *Sphagnum* mosses, plants that contain numerous cells empty of protoplasm and serve only to store water. They can absorb 20 times their own weight of liquid, and this property has enabled them to be used as emergency dressings in times of war.

In spite of their wet habitat, *Sphagnums* owe their existence to their capacity to retain water. Lacking roots, the entire plant must absorb water and mineral salts from its environment. A supply of essential nutrients is assured when the plant is immersed in water, but *Sphagnums* grow to form elevated humps and are then reliant on moisture obtained from the air, such as rain or dew. Where extensive growth of *Sphagnum* leads to the development of a raised bog, the moss offers a suitable habitat for other plants, and on one of these I recognized the reddish, circular leaves of the sundew. Nutrition is poor in acid bogs, but the sundew has evolved a mode of life that makes it largely independent of the base on which it grows.

It is carnivorous. Reddish glandular hairs on its leaves are death-traps for insects. Some hairs give off an odour that attracts insects, but once the prey has alighted on the plant, other sticky hairs curl round and hold the insect to the leaf where it is slowly digested by a secretion of enzymes.

The sundew's grisly feeding habit is made possible by the large numbers of insects that live on the vidda. Midges, gnats and blackflies swarm around the bogs, although in terms of sheer numbers and unpleasantness, they are insignificant compared with mosquitoes, the curse of the Lapland plateau. Ever since leaving the car I had been a target for these bloodsuckers. But as I made my way round their boggy breeding grounds, they rose to meet me in dark, swirling clouds, insinuating themselves in my clothes, choking my mouth and smothering every inch of my skin in bites. As I saw my hands beginning to swell, I ruefully consoled myself with the thought that at least I would not contract malaria, because my tormenters belonged to the genus *Aedes*, which, happily, are not carriers of the disease.

That is small comfort to those who have suffered a sustained attack by mosquitoes. And insect repellents are only partially successful deterrents because as soon as the victim begins to sweat, the repellent loses

Lured to a sundew plant by its sweet scent, an insect is trapped by the plant's sticky leaf-hairs, which trap the victim while the plant secretes digestive enzymes and devours it. The sundew, which grows in acid peat bogs, relies on insects for its essential nutriment.

most of its effectiveness. In any case, it is not body odours that first attract the mosquitoes. Research has shown that the insects are alerted to the presence of a potential meal by a rise in the concentration of carbon dioxide in the air, such as would be caused by the breath of any warm-blooded creature. Randomly at first, the mosquitoes tack back and forth across this zone until they reach a spot that shows a relative increase in warmth and humidity. They can detect a difference in air temperature of only one-five-hundredth of a degree F, and once they have locked on to the heat waves, they follow them to their source and begin feeding.

Not everyone is vulnerable to mosquito bites. Occasionally the insects will divert their flight away from an intended target, apparently repelled by some odour given off by the victim's sweat. One such fortunate person was subjected to a series of experiments by scientists working to produce a foolproof insect repellent. First, he was placed in a room containing a swarm of mosquitoes that were thirsting for blood. He emerged with only two bites, and was then placed in a steam bath until he had produced three and a half pints of sweat. This was collected and analysed for whatever substance it contained that repelled the mosquitoes.

Not enough information was gained from this experiment. But from such research may one day come an effective repellent. Until then the only reliable method of combating the mosquito menace is to tackle the problem at its source—the bogs and pools that are the mosquitoes' breeding grounds. Thin films of oil sprayed on to the surface of the ponds prevent the larvae, which hang from the surface, from breathing, and they perish. D.D.T., one of the chlorinated hydrocarbon insecticides, kills mosquitoes by inhibiting their nervous systems.

Its use has been credited with the eradication of malaria and other mosquito-borne diseases in many parts of the world. Unfortunately, D.D.T. and its residues are also absorbed by other animals that prey on the contaminated mosquitoes, and because the chemicals are not broken down in the predators' bodies, they are passed on, in ever greater concentrations, to animals at the top of the food chain. These birds are rarely killed outright by D.D.T. poisoning, but sub-lethal doses of the chemicals cause some eggs to have abnormally thin shells that break during the incubation period. So far the Lapland wilderness has escaped the massive D.D.T. pollution that has virtually wiped out such species as the peregrine falcon in England and the bald eagle and osprey in the eastern U.S. But, already, Finnish ornithologists are reporting very poor breeding records of peregrines in their country, and they lay the blame on the increasing use of chlorinated hydrocarbon insecticides.

Those people who believe that mosquitoes should be wiped out should consider that, apart from the danger presented to the Lapland environment by the chemical elimination of mosquitoes, these insects are an important food for many of the birds that breed on the boggy plateau. What brought this fact home to me was the sight of a bird—the first I had seen since leaving the car—swimming buoyantly on a sedgy pool near the edge of the bogs. The bird was a wader, no more than seven inches long, and the sides of its neck and head were a warm russet colour. But much more eye-catching than its plumage were the peculiar movements the bird was making. As it swam, its head nodded like that of a clockwork toy, and occasionally it stopped its forward motion and pirouetted daintily in the water, working its legs vigorously as it did so.

The bird was a red-necked phalarope, and the purpose of its strange behaviour was to disturb bottom-dwelling larvae and insects and bring them to the surface to feed on them. I had never seen this species before, but I already knew that the rest of the bird's habits are as unusual as its feeding method. For a start, the sexual roles are reversed in this species. The female (it was a female I had seen) is the more brightly coloured of the sexes and takes the lead during courtship and breeding. When she has laid her eggs, the male takes over incubation and care of the young, while the female defends the territory. Sometimes, however, she courts another male and lays a second clutch of eggs. Precisely what purpose this role reversal achieves is unclear; but it could be that, freed of the time-consuming task of rising and caring for young, the female is able to lay an unusually large number of eggs during the brief arctic summer and thus produce a surplus population of chicks.

A surplus population is necessary for the survival of the species, for not only do many individuals fall prey to predators but their numbers are seriously depleted during their migratory flights to and from their winter feeding grounds off the coast of north-west Africa. Among the hazards with which they must contend along their route are storms, unseen obstructions such as power cables, and ambushing hawks and falcons; yet each spring, breeding birds return to Lapland in the same numbers. Almost all Lapland's birds undertake equally risky journeys. Some, like the birds of prey, make comparatively short journeys to more temperate parts of Europe. Others, like the ring-ouzel, a northern cousin of the blackbird, reach North Africa. But quite a few of the vidda species, mostly waders like the golden plover, whimbrel and little stint cross the Equator.

What compels these birds to undertake such long, hazardous migrations is not in doubt: arctic winters are so severe and dark that diurnal birds that feed on insects or vegetation must, with very few exceptions, move south or starve. We also know that birds are stimulated to migrate by secretions of hormones from the endocrine glands (which also control breeding and egg-laying behaviour) and that these glands are in turn stimulated by seasonal changes in the quantity and quality of sunlight. What is not known with certainty is the original cause of migratory behaviour or how a bird can navigate with such remarkable precision halfway round the world.

So much of Lapland's wildlife owes its nature, distribution and behaviour to the effects of the Pleistocene Ice Ages that it is tempting to see in the phenomenon of migration a behavioural line with a period when birds were forced south by the advancing ice sheets, returning to their ancestral homes when the ice retreated. But this does not explain why birds in parts of the world that were never touched by ice also migrate. A more logical explanation is that birds originating in warm climates started to migrate millions of years before the Pleistocene period. Spreading outwards in their search for food, many found it in higher latitudes but were forced to withdraw when winter came. While some of these pioneers perished, the more flexible individuals survived to establish regular migration patterns.

There is much less certainty about how birds navigate with such precision on their migratory flights. How, for example, can the little stint, an arctic wader only eight inches long, survive the rigours of a 7,000-mile journey from South Africa and still land on its previous year's nest on the vidda? The most widely accepted of a multitude of theories is that the birds rely on visual landmarks such as rivers and mountains, using the sun as a compass. There is also evidence that nocturnal migrants navigate by the stars alone. And yet, when I took a last look at the phalarope and imagined the thousands of miles and countless dangers it would have to face before returning next spring to the vidda, I could not help thinking that mere scientific explanations could never do justice to such an extraordinary achievement.

Returning to the car, I resumed my journey to Kautokeino. As I drove farther south the land on each side of the road gradually lost its barren, windswept character. The bare summits of some fells still formed stark silhouettes against the sky, but the outlines of many others were blurred by a stubble of trees. Where the road ran beside the river Alta, it cut between groves of birches, and as it dipped down to the hollow where

Spring thaw leaves a birchwood in the vidda a tangle of sodden tussocks and dead vegetation. Although precipitation over the plateau is low during most of the year, winter snowfalls are heavy, and when the snow thaws meltwater inundates low-lying areas, rising to waist height in some places.

Kautokeino nestles, I saw that the birches ran for miles up the valleys to the north and south of the village.

It was in one of these valleys, formed by one of the Alta's many tributaries that, next day, I explored this new and gentler face of the vidda. Walking south from Kautokeino in the morning, I left the straggle of buildings behind in a few minutes. Soon after crossing a bridge that spanned the tributary, I was in the middle of a birch forest. "Forest" is perhaps a misleading word, for these birches were not the tall, slim trees of temperate regions. Instead they had become stunted and dwarfed so as to survive the harsh conditions. Although their thin, drooping branches looked frail, when I tried to break one it proved as tough as wire, and when a breeze stirred the trees I saw how the branches flailed the surrounding vegetation.

In spite of their contorted appearance, the birches had a special kind of beauty, as delicate as a Japanese brush painting. Their papery pale stems were decorated by darker patches that looked like inscriptions in some unknown block cipher, and because the thin leaf cover did not entirely blot out the sky, the sun created ever-shifting patterns of light and shade on the forest floor. The beauty of these trees is short-lived, however: birches rarely live longer than a hundred years—a short span compared with other trees—and most succumb to fungal attack long before. Many of these birches, did, in fact, support colonies of fungi, and when I examined the growths more closely, I recognized the smooth lobes of *Polyporus betulinus*, or razor-strop fungus, so-called because it was once used to strop cut-throat razors. Sprouting from the moss under some trees were the vivid red- and white-spotted caps of fly agaric, a poisonous toadstool employed by tribes in eastern Siberia as a powerful hallucinogen.

In places the forest was broken up by bogs and clearings that supported a much richer ground flora than I had seen on the treeless plateau. Grasses and ferns grew tall, and in their shade, absorbing nutrition from their roots, was the red-stemmed, yellow-flowered moor king plant. It was named King Charles's sceptre by its Swedish discoverer, in honour of his monarch's victory over the Russians in 1700, and another famous Swede, Linnaeus, once wrote a thesis on it. But, he noted sadly, someone else "has received the credit for it". This may have prompted him to list the moor king less flatteringly as a species of *Pedicularis*, or lousewort.

In the glades it was easy to imagine that somehow I had been transported to some woodland clearing in southern England. Yet the profusion of plants on the wooded vidda creates an illusory impression of fertility; within a few weeks, as autumn arrived, the flowers would blacken and wither, the grasses and ferns would shrivel up, and almost overnight the birches would be stripped of their leaves.

It was on another visit to the vidda that I saw how quickly autumn turned to winter. September mist hung over the river and hugged the floors of the surrounding valleys rising out of it, the birch forests stretched to the horizon in a conflagration of colour. As if in compensation for their stunted growth, each tree was decked in flaming colours that ranged from palest yellow to deepest red, and on the forest floor, the ferns, grasses and berries glowed like embers.

The spectacle was soon over, however. A few days later I awoke to see a light dusting of snow on the summits of the fells, and all through the following week the normally silent vidda rustled with the sound of leaves falling through the branches. Each morning the sun rose a little later and shone less strongly; and each evening it set a little earlier. Day by day there were fewer leaves on the trees, and the snow crept down from the hills, until, one morning, it blanketed the entire landscape.

Winter had not fully descended yet, however. The midday sun continued to shine with a sickly yellow light that threw the bare birch branches into stark relief, and animals were still reaping the last fruits of the brief autumn. Walking in the woods, I disturbed family parties of willow tits picking birch seeds from the snow, and once I flushed a willow grouse from the pit it had dug for warmth in the snow. But few birds remained in the forest, and many that did were seasonal invaders from the high plateau, like the ptarmigan I surprised feeding on what little vegetation still protruded above the snow. Each night the sky was noisy with the clamour of wildfowl flying south in endless skeins, until by the end of October almost all the migrants had left and the only night sound was the hooting of owls from the forest.

The onset of winter had driven most birds south, but the mammals remained on the vidda and, judging by the wealth of tracks that crisscrossed the snow, in numbers that I had never before suspected. I discovered that, with practice, I could read whole diaries from the tracks, and it was by following the trail of an arctic hare that I unexpectedly encountered an animal I had often sought but never seen.

I picked up the hare's trail on the fringe of the forest, where it had been scraping in the snow for the plants that lay beneath. From here, the trail led into a birch thicket, and I could tell from the short distance that separated each set of prints that the hare had been moving casually, at a steady lope. Before leaving the thicket, it had stopped to eat the tip of a young birch, leaving the stump obliquely sliced through with the precision of garden shears. Another animal had already attacked the tree: for a height of two or three inches above the snow, the bark had been neatly stripped away, probably by one of the smallest rodents of the vidda, the ruddy vole.

At the edge of the thicket, a single set of prints revealed that the hare had paused. Instead of the two prints of the forefeet appearing behind the hindfeet, as happens when the hare is moving, the forefeet made light impressions just in front of the hindfeet, indicating that the hare had squatted on its hindquarters, watching for possible danger before leaving the safety of the thicket. Then the tracks changed once again, the distance between each set of prints and the depth of the rear prints indicating that the hare had crossed the open ground at a gallop. Halfway across the clearing, the hare's trail was crossed by that of a stoat.

In the soft snow the stoat had moved in a succession of jumps, placing its hindfeet in the tracks of its forefeet, so that the prints appeared in pairs. I could not tell which trail had been made first, but perhaps the hare had scented its enemy because, just after the trails crossed, the hare turned, retraced its own tracks for a distance, then made a large jump to one side—a manoeuvre that seemed to have fooled the stoat, for its tracks went off in a different direction.

I continued to follow the hare's trail. By following it I had learned in a few minutes what a week's patient observation in summer could not have revealed. I had already gained a new insight into the arctic hare's feeding habits, its shyness and its stratagems for confusing predators. But I never expected to catch up with my quarry—I did not even know whether the trail was five minutes or two days old. So I was taken aback when, emerging from a thick clump of birches into a rock-strewn clearing, I saw the hare only a few paces ahead of me.

It was stretched out on the snow, quite dead, surrounded by its entrails and a vivid patch of blood. Beside it, lips drawn back from bloody teeth in a soundless snarl, crouched its killer, a full-grown wolverine. I had heard and read a great deal about this animal, the largest and most rapacious of the weasel family. I had heard of its wanton destructiveness, its ability to rip a hole in a log cabin to get at the food within. The Lapps had told me how the wolverine will lie in wait on a tree branch for a reindeer, then drop down from above and bite its victim's spinal cord. I had read of the wolverine's gluttonous appetite, and of the way it will bite through its own toes to free them from a trap. These and other stories I had tended to dismiss as exaggerated if not downright fanciful.

A wolverine, conspicuous in the snow, emerges from its lair. But it has little need of winter camouflage, for no other animal will attack it.

But now that I was face to face with a specimen, I was not so sure.

The beast was much larger than I had expected, over three feet long and powerfully built, with short, thick-set legs and a relatively narrow, snake-like head that seemed all mouth and teeth. It looked more like a small bear than a giant weasel, and the impression was reinforced when it raised its hackles and emitted a low, throaty growl. But what impressed me most was its fearlessness. On seeing me the wolverine did not give an inch and we must have stared at each other for a full 20 seconds before, almost nonchalantly, it turned its back on me and lolloped back into the forest. I did not follow it.

Only later did I realize how rare my chance encounter had been. Wolverines are public enemy number one on the reindeer pastures around Kautokeino, and only their native cunning and nocturnal habits have ensured that they are still widespread, if uncommon, on the vidda. The wolf has not been so lucky. Shot at from helicopters and snow scooters, poisoned by baited carcases, it has now been reduced to some ten breeding pairs throughout the whole of Norwegian Lapland, a resident population that is swollen in the winter by wolves that cross over the Russian border and reach the vidda through Finland. I never saw one of these beasts or came across any of their tracks, nor did I hear the wildest sound to be heard in Lapland: the doleful howl of a wolf echoing across the snowy, moonlit vidda.

Perhaps it is because there are so few wolves that the elk, which until a century ago did not live on the Lapland plateau, can now be seen in the birch forests. Occasionally I did come across their tracks and found saplings that they had broken down in their efforts to reach the higher, more succulent branches. Like the wolverine, the elk has been the subject of so many myths that it is difficult to separate fact from fiction. Pliny the Elder, the Roman natural historian, originated some of the myths. He believed that the elk had no knees and was forced to sleep standing up, leaning against a tree. According to him, all a hunter had to do was to chop down the tree and the elk would fall helplessly to the ground. Other writers believed that the elk suffered from a form of epilepsy that it cured by opening a vein behind its ear with a hind foot. Others maintained that the elk's upper lip was so large that the beast could graze only by walking backwards.

It all seems ridiculous until you meet an elk, and then you are prepared to believe almost anything about this strange-looking mammal. You first notice its great bearded head, topped by a massive spread of palmate antlers that can be six feet across. The head is supported on bulging, humped shoulders that slope back to weak-looking hind-quarters and an apology of a tail. You are not surprised to see that the upper lip is pendulous, giving the animal a downcast, mournful look, and that the long, gangly legs appear incapable of supporting the body. But then watch the same animal in motion, and its comically sad aura is dispelled. Its long legs propel it effortlessly at a ground-eating lope, and its feet are tipped with razor-sharp hoofs that can split open the skull of a wolf. The shaggy door-mat coat is a superb insulator. The oversized ears and snout provide early warning of any predators foolish enough to come within striking distance of those formidable hoofs.

On that visit to the vidda, I left before mid-winter. The sun still rose for a few hours each day, but its feeble rays barely illuminated a world that had been bleached of all colour; and in the profound silence of the birch forest, I felt the *mørkeskye*—the depression that afflicts those who must overwinter in the arctic darkness. I was not anxious to experience this sensation at any length, so I left Lapland to wait until May and the coming of spring. Its arrival on the vidda was sudden. One morning the ice broke up on the river Alta with a grating roar and was followed by the sound of running water. Later, rain fell, melting the snow in patches, creating a landscape of stark, black-and-white contrasts, like the images on a photographic negative.

In the forest clearings, flowers sprang up within days, sometimes hours, of the melting of the snow. Brilliant yellow marsh marigolds thrust through dead grass made sodden by streams of meltwater; winter-green, globe flowers and the rare Lapland *Oxytropis* grew in dense carpets. Some days, however, this sudden regrowth was temporarily halted by fresh squalls of snow sweeping down from the fells. Lapland winters give up their hold on the land reluctantly, and it was not until I saw the delicate new leaves of the birches emerging and heard the cries of the wildfowl passing overhead that I knew spring had returned to the vidda, a luxurious prelude to the fierce and fleeting intensity of summer.

Pioneering Impressions

In the 16th Century a Swedish priest, Olaus Magnus, travelled extensively through the wildest parts of northern Scandinavia, including Lapland. Although the object of his mission was to heal religious differences brought about by the Reformation, he also seized on the opportunity to study the area's rich and prolific wildlife.

Some years later Sweden became Protestant and Magnus chose to spend the remainder of his life outside his own country. He used the years of self-imposed exile in Catholic Europe to collate and write up the extensive material he had gathered on his journeys in the northern wilderness, and in 1555 he published his *Historia de Gentibus septentrionalibus*, or *Treatise Concerning the Northern Peoples*.

While the work concentrated on people Magnus had met in his wanderings, it was none the less remarkable for its studies of flora and fauna. Some of the book's illustrations—possibly drawn by the author himself—are reproduced on the following pages.

Not all of the comments and drawings stand up to modern scientific scrutiny, partly because Magnus attached religious explanations to natural phenomena and partly because he acquired part of his information through hearsay. He showed lemmings, for example, pouring out of the sky, and rendered many sea creatures larger than life to dramatize the hazards they posed to fishermen.

Recalling his own experience of the merciless Lapland climate, Magnus wrote of the innumerable animals that also felt its piercing cold. And of the dangers of poor visibility during winter, he said: "So great sometimes is the force of the frosts and the falling snow in the Northern parts, and so sharp are the tempests and vehement darkness . . . that travellers cannot . . . know the next man that comes, be he friend or foe."

What most impressed Magnus, however, was the fact that so many creatures managed to survive in the cruellest conditions and rear their young. With admiration, he remarked: "When they are shut in on all sides with snow and ice, and no food to be found on the ground, they will not only live, but bring forth young ones and feed them, and amid the sharpest elements take no harm."

A decorative page from Olaus Magnus's 16th-Century Latin work (right) includes both a description of the "lynces", or lynx, and a woodcut showing two of the animals hunting their favourite prey, wild cat. Lynx "never look back", he wrote, "but always run and leap forward".

De Lyncibus, & pellibus eorundem.

CAP. XII.

Lynces aquilonares.

Lyncurium.

Opinio succini generati refellitur.

Natura lyncis.

Pelles lyncinæ.

Pelles i frigore meliores.

YNCES in Septentrionalibus syluis non adeó frequentes generantur, vt lupi , licet impares haud sint in auiditate prædarum . Quòd autem Plinius lib. VIII. cap. XXXVIII. asserit, eorum vrina gemmam lyncurium vocatam, instarǫ carbunculi rutilantem, humi defossam generari , atque jn succinum conuerti , verisimile non videtur, vt cùm hæc bestia aliis inuidens, vrinam suam arena, vel terra opertam , profundius claudat : quò nunquàm peruenium muscæ, ranæ, araneæ, vermes , bruchi, culices, neque formicæ: quæ passim in succino omnium colore variato , inclusæ videntur, prout superius lib. XII. cap. VIII. IX. ac XX. diffusius est ostensum. Nec lyncum transitus est prope riuos, vel aquas, sed campos, & syluas: vnde lyncurium, siue succinum inde generatum ad mare , & deinde vi tempestatum in tot millibus librarum, in littora Prutenica detrudi , & colligi posse, credibile non sit. Natura igitur lyncis est, vt non respiciat retrò, sed continuo progressu, & saltu præcipitet cursum. Cibus illi syluestrium cattorum frequentior, aut suauior est: quia sicut illis libentius vescitur, ita & eorum latibulis, vt rapiat, insidiatur . Pelles eius mollioribus plumis , & pulchrioribus maculis præditæ , satis carè venduntur , præsertim in asperrima hyeme prædatæ: tunc enim in virtute , & colore sunt aptiores, vti æstate viliores, immò deteriores. Qualiter autem & hæ , & aliæ pelles falsificentur , videat qui velit, supradicto VI. lib. cap. vltimo .

A Laplander astride a tame reindeer uses his whip to drive wild reindeer into captivity. Magnus was greatly impressed by the usefulness of these creatures, referring to "their Milk, Skins, Sinews, Bones, Hoofs, Horns, Hair and dainty Flesh to feed on".

Firs, pines, junipers and larches, resplendent with cones and fruit, illustrate the variety of trees to be found in the northern woods. Magnus noted that the tips of the pines were collected "by the Laplanders, who gathering them in Summer, eat them for bread".

Their coats changing from summer brown to white with the onset of winter, two hares "feed on the Pine-Tree Bark". Until Magnus made this observation, it was widely believed that Lapland hares fed on snow and that this enabled them to take on their winter camouflage.

Surging up from the deep, dogfish—members of the shark family—attack an imprudent swimmer off the northern coast. They are being attacked, in turn, by a ray that, "with some violence drives away these fish and doth what he can to urge (the man) to swim out".

Allowing himself some poetic licence, Magnus shows an outsize polypus—a kind of lobster—grabbing an over-inquisitive Lapland fisherman. Near by, curled up and feeding, another lobster "casts out the shells of crabs", while others scour the sea-bed for food.

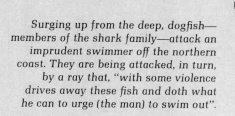

A wily red fox "fishes" with its tail for crabs off the Lapland coast. At the same time the fox rids itself of water-hating fleas that hop from its body on to the grass held in its jaws. Another fox that has been feigning death catches the birds that "come down unawares".

Deprived of other prey by the harsh winter, a pack of hungry wolves surges round a horse-drawn sleigh of travellers who "must drive them off with bows and guns". Occasionally, Lapland's wolves raided houses, Magnus reported, dragging cattle off into the forest.

Perched on the upper branches of snow-laden trees, "snow-birds" watch for birds of prey. The "snow-birds" cannot be identified from Magnus's description, but he reported that when they spotted their enemy, "they thrust themselves into the snow for protection".

Fleeing from a marksman's bow, three outsized red squirrels display ear-tufts of varied size. Magnus found that the farther north the squirrels were, the thicker would be their fur, "the cold being the cause", and drew varying ear-tufts to convey this difference.

Cornered after a hard chase, sables and martens turn ferociously upon their pursuers. Magnus pointed out that the two species were always very difficult to distinguish in the wild, explaining that it was only "by the quality of their Skins" that they could be told apart.

Magnus explained periodic increases in lemming population by showing them falling from a rain cloud. According to his hearsay account, they "destroy all green things, and all dies they bite on". But the voracious lemmings, he noted, were themselves "devoured by beasts".

An "eagle" pounces on a hare to feed its young, hidden in rocks near by. Although various birds of prey exist in Lapland, "by reason of the abundance of Wild Beasts" on which to feed, Magnus called them all eagles except the gyr falcon, the "most noble Bird of all".

4/ The Legendary Lemmings

This land has an extraordinary pest, which the Norwegians in their own language call "leem" or "lemmer" . . . During storms and sudden rains these creatures fall down to earth.

JAKOB ZIEGLER/ QUAE INTUS CONTINENTUR (1532)

It was a day in late summer a few years ago when lemmings, moving down from their usual remote habitats among the northern hills of Norway, surprised local inhabitants by appearing on the streets of Fauske, the northern terminal of the Nordland railway. At first they came in small numbers, but soon there were thousands of them—so many, in fact, that dogs tired of killing them. The lemmings would no doubt have continued on their way had it not been for the railway line that crossed their route.

Here the lemmings halted, suspicious and increasingly nervous, and soon built up into a huge concentration beside the tracks. In such a situation, packed closely together, migrating lemmings can be seized by panic; and unaware of danger and death may begin a desperate rush. This is what happened at Fauske.

Some made the break and soon hundreds of them swarmed across the tracks. Just then a train approached, but the lemmings continued to cross. The train ploughed through them, killing so many that the engine had to be hosed down to remove the stains of slaughter.

The following month another migration reached Fauske fjord, this time from the hills and ridges to the south. At the fjord there was the usual hesitation and caution that lemmings display when they have to cross water; then they started to swim. Some perished because the widest part of the fjord was too much for them, and others were drowned in the strong current flowing through a gullet, although a few were carried ashore by eddies.

Those lemmings that made use of the road and rail bridge over the fjord suffered an even more bizarre fate. In their customary manner, the lemmings scuttled from one side of the bridge to the other instead of proceeding straight ahead. A fair proportion crossed safely, but then, as the bridge became crowded, those in the middle panicked. They could not turn back because of the press behind them and they suddenly refused to go on. They sought to escape the dilemma by scampering to the edge and desperately flinging themselves off. Those that fell to the ground were killed; those that fell into the water fared little better, for the rapids swept most of them away and the gulls that day had a rare feast.

These two accounts of lemming behaviour fall a little short of the popular tales of migrations that are said to end in wretched suicide in the cold northern seas. That is the lemming of legend and folklore. The lemmings of my experience do not dash recklessly in formation across country and I believe they have no wish for self-destruction. My interest in lemmings began in childhood when I read stories about their mysterious behaviour in the wild arctic. I readily accepted the popular idea that migrating lemmings poured across the snow and through the pine forests, sticking to their chosen route to the sea in spite of all obstacles. It was only in adult life, when I decided to do some serious research on lemmings and wrote for information to newspapers in Scandinavia, that I began to doubt whether lemmings ran into the sea at all! Migrations ending in this way proved, in fact, to be the very rare exception rather than the rule. But my years of collecting information about lemmings, of visiting lemming country and of observing the creatures at close range have done nothing to diminish my interest in them, for their actual behaviour is as fascinating as any ascribed to them by legend.

The colourful legends, of course, take little account of the lemmings' importance to other creatures of the wilderness. Lemmings are perhaps the most widely known, most interesting and typical Lapland animal. They are such vital links in the food chain that few predators would be able to survive for long in their absence. The lemmings depend upon vegetation for their food, and the predators, in turn, eat the lemmings. Even a temporary scarcity of lemmings will seriously affect the rest of the animal population. Fur trappers, for example, report that their catches of valuable fur-bearing animals, including foxes and ermines, show a marked drop when the lemming population is in decline. The Laplanders also find that some of their own sources of food, such as grouse and hares, are in short supply at such periods, having fallen victims to predators that otherwise would have fed on the lemmings.

Most Laplanders, however, regard lemmings in much the way that city dwellers regard rats: as destructive and distasteful pests. The idea that I had come all the way from Britain to study lemmings was regarded as mildly eccentric, if not downright foolish. Some people showed little curiosity about them, while others displayed repugnance, fear, or even superstitious terror. Several times I was warned that the lemming bite is poisonous and lethal. Like so many other stories told about these animals, this is not true.

For more than 300 years outbreaks of disease have also been attributed to the stench of rotting lemming corpses. Lemmings die in great numbers in spring when their habitats are liable to be flooded by melt water, or from epidemic diseases. Others may starve to death in winter. Until the end of the last century it was thought that lemmings were responsible for outbreaks of scarlet fever, and even nowadays they are believed to cause tularemia, or "lemming fever", which has symptoms akin to plague. In 1960 and again in 1961 lemming fever was said to have broken out near Fauske. Gastro-enteritis was eventually diagnosed, which itself could well have been caused by the many drowned lemmings that were found in the water supply on both occasions.

The lemming is soft, well padded and pretty—and much smaller than is generally supposed. An adult lemming will normally measure less than four inches from whisker to the sprout that passes for a tail, and weigh about two ounces—compared with 17 to 34 ounces for a guinea-pig. And while the lack of a chin and the two very long and sharp teeth behind the incised upper lip prevent the lemming from attaining ideal beauty, there is compensation.

For its glossy brown coat, richly patterned with black on the upper parts and yellow along the neck, is a handsomely striking feature. The sides are tawny and the underparts much paler, from buff to nearly white. (The attractive markings, however, hold no special interest for the fur trade. The Hudson's Bay Company long ago decided that the animal had no commercial value since the skin—a tender parchment—lacks durability.) The ears are scarcely visible, the eyes small, round and black. On the ground the lemming's movements are jerky and hesitant, its short legs and plump rump giving it a rather comical charm. But it is agile and I have noticed how it can swerve with speed to avoid capture.

The lemming I have described is the Norwegian lemming, *Lemmus*

Taking a defensive stance, a tiny Norwegian lemming crouches low in the grass. In spite of its size it reacts aggressively when threatened. The lemming will often attack first, snarling with bared teeth and lunging forward to snap at a supposed enemy.

lemmus, the biggest and most famous of a dozen lemming species that are found in various parts of the arctic world. The Norwegian lemming was present in Britain during the last Ice Age, which ended some 10,000 years ago, and it even ranged as far south as Portugal. This lemming and the arctic fox are thought by many zoologists to be the only mammals to have survived in Scandinavia from pre-glacial times.

It is usually very difficult to find lemmings in any one place, but at regular intervals—known as lemming years—they appear in vast numbers, then die off just as assuredly. This curious fluctuation has puzzled men for centuries. A neat explanation was given by a Bavarian geographer named Jakob Ziegler, who published the first account of lemmings in 1532. He had met two successive Norwegian archbishops in Rome and they told him that lemmings were generated from foul matter in the clouds, falling to earth in stormy weather. In 1555 a Swedish archbishop, Olaus Magnus, published the first illustration of lemmings, and actually showed them falling from clouds.

It was not until 1771 that an English traveller, Thomas Pennant, offered a less fanciful explanation. He believed that lemmings migrated regularly from Russia's Kola Peninsula through Finnmark, the northern-most province of Norway. But the earlier theory persisted and as late as 1847 one distinguished Norwegian professor was unable to "discover anything unreasonable in this explanation". There are still people who believe in this descent from the clouds and the idea is not confined to Scandinavia. Some Eskimos share the belief, referring to one species of lemming as "the creature from space".

The peak lemming time occurs every three or four years. Lemmings are then seen in large numbers, usually in the spring but sometimes through to autumn. No one can tell you exactly where to find lemmings in summer, as I know only too well. I have set off post-haste after being assured that they were plentiful in some spot, only to discover on arrival that I was too late. But on the occasions when they proliferate I have known them to dash out, yelping and snapping at my boots as I approached, sometimes before I even realized they were there.

When angry, they often sit up on their hindquarters, their fur erect, and may bob up and down, hissing and squealing; or they may crouch, ready to spring, snarling, teeth bared. Sometimes they make a strange, almost continuous guttural churring sound deep in the throat. I have known occasions when a cornered lemming has leapt at my hand, biting at my glove, its grip so powerful that it hung on even when lifted several feet off the ground. They will also lock their jaws on to a stick, allowing themselves to be pulled out of a hole or crevice rather than let go.

The lemming will often display a surprising lack of caution. It gives away its whereabouts with a combination of furious yelps and growls, and instead of fleeing before a superior foe will stand its ground and even attack first. Lemmings, it seems, feel threatened by large moving objects, and use attack as the best means of defence. They have gone for me while I was cycling, and they will spring at a dog, a reindeer or even a car. In fact, they will attack almost anything that moves, provided it is bigger than them. When several voles were placed with some lemmings, the lemmings did not react, but the voles did: they fled!

Lemmings not only attack intruders and enemies, real and presumed; they also fight frequently among themselves when numbers are high. Two mature males will box and grapple and chase and bite, although rarely to the death. Female lemmings display even greater aggression, fighting not only one another but frequently attacking males with unbelievable savagery when unready or unwilling to mate. As the males nearly always refrain from biting in these sexual tussles, the females invariably win. There is also much persecution of young animals by their elders, even parents.

And yet one experienced observer has written: "By nature the lemming is timid, suspicious, not without reason, and as a consequence extremely cautious." That does not sound like all the lemmings I have met, but it is none the less generally true. We seem to be dealing with a Jekyll and Hyde of the animal world, for lemmings behave very differently in normal years from years when they are numerous. Usually they do not range far from their territories and warily take advantage of cover on their feeding paths through vegetation. A terrain perfect for lemmings in all respects is at Lake Kilpisjärvi, where Finland and Sweden reach up to the Norwegian border, south of Lygenfjord. Here the mountains, rising to more than 4,500 feet, are among the highest in Finland. Reflected in the lake is the 3,380-foot peak of Saana, plunging through the clouds like the prow and deck of an aircraft carrier.

I knew that in a good year lemmings could be found here and I made a search from the lake shore to a height of about 2,000 feet, where the vegetation gives way to grasses and sedges. I began to climb from the tide-line of spring floods on the narrow rocky shore, pushing through birches mingled with junipers, crowberries and bilberries, past ferns and globe flowers, by thickets and past hummocks of bog where sphagnum predominates and scented rose-root provides welcome splashes of red and yellow.

A short-tailed grey vole pursues its restless search for edible vegetation in Lapland's open scrub. Like the lemming, this species experiences periodical increases in numbers that set off mass migrations. Sometimes the vole population swells so dramatically that it approaches plague proportions.

I was looking for ground soft enough for lemmings to burrow in but not too wet for comfort and where berry bushes, lichens and mosses provided plenty of cover. Lemmings will tunnel among the roots of trees and shrubs or from a natural hole between stones to make summer nests. Taking care to avoid some particularly repellent quaking bogs, I prodded about among thickets of dwarf birches and junipers and investigated tussocks, peat hummocks and shoals that I knew provided typical nesting sites. For from this shelter lemmings could easily make runways into the sedges and grasses where they feed.

Lemmings are wasteful feeders, discarding the upper parts of grasses and leaves after only a nibble, and I soon found signs of their presence. Scattered on the ground near some bushes and a fallen birch were bits of juniper twigs and bilberry stems, clear evidence that a lemming had been dining there. And what a charming sight it would have made. A lemming bites off leaves or grass, then sits up on its hind legs, holding the food in its forepaws—sometimes one paw. The pose I liked best was when I once saw a lemming perched with its meal on a mushroom cap.

The lemming normally sticks to a vegetarian diet and has been described by the Oxford ecologist, Charles Elton, as a fat, busy, agile mowing machine. About one-third of its weight is packed in its gut. It will eat up to twice its own weight of food every 24 hours. In a year, then, this creature, which itself weighs no more than a couple of ounces, can eat one hundredweight of vegetation. I have seen what a lemming colony can do to a stretch of marshy ground thickly covered with herbage. By the time the lemmings had been through it, it looked like muddy wasteland devastated by the trampling boots of an army. All the plants had disappeared and where previously there had been grass tussocks, only lumps of earth remained. Mounds of droppings, some of them several inches high, were scattered throughout the area.

The whole question of lemming voracity and its effect on vegetation causes much disputation among experts who are not Lapps. The Lapps have no doubt at all. They claim that the lemmings make serious inroads into the supply of reindeer lichen and, after a good deal of investigation, I believe the Lapps are right.

Although lemmings will happily gorge themselves on vegetation found in their native arctic habitat, exotic foods can bring fatal results. At one zoo that shall be nameless, a lemming died after being fed on pineapple. They are not popular animals with zoos and there is now none at any zoo that I know of. This is probably because they do not

Lichen-covered rocks on the shore of Lake Kilpisjärvi, in Finnish Lapland, form one of the favourite departure points for lemmings on their migration across this expanse of water. Slithering hesitantly down the rocks and into the water, the lemmings, guided by their keen eyesight, strike out for the far bank.

display well for the public—they are small and unspectacular, tend to be most active after sunset and like to hide from view.

It is often assumed that they will not survive captivity. This is not so. I recall a hair-raising pursuit of a lemming across the roofs of central London after it had escaped at night from the flat of a friend. This lemming and a companion had been brought from Norway and both flourished in their new environment for more than a year.

They helped to corroborate an observation of mine. In Swedish Lapland I had watched a lemming in a thicket of dwarf willows where it paddled contentedly through melt water, feeding at intervals. It put its face into the water at one point, then tilted its head and went through much the same gulping motions as a domestic fowl after drinking. The actions were quite different from those of swallowing food, which I had been able to watch over three days on that occasion. Some naturalists strongly challenged my findings, insisting that the lemming was sure to have been eating, for in their opinion lemmings do not drink at all but take whatever moisture they need from their food.

The London lemmings, however, readily drank water. They not only drank from the teat of a bottle but also squeezed the teat with their forepaws, licking up the few drops that then fell on the grass of their cage. Other lemmings have also been seen to drink without hesitation.

Lemmings do not hibernate but live in tunnels under the winter snow, where they rely on moss, grass, sedge and other herbage that remains green. They forage under the snow until spring, seldom venturing above the surface. No food is stored against the possibility of hardship, and if food is not available near by the lemmings die.

I have studied lemming tunnels in Swedish Lapland at the onset of winter. The animals begin construction work by butting, scraping with the forepaws and throwing back the snow with the hind feet. They prefer to start from a snowdrift formed in the shelter of a boulder, hummock or shrub, for they need about a yard's depth of snow, not always available because gales often clear the ground or leave only a thin covering. Most tunnels are about a dozen yards long, ending blindly; and here the lemmings make their round winter nest with a small entrance hole at the side. Tunnel and nest are generally free of droppings, for short side tunnels may be used as latrines and it is usual to find large heaps of droppings, looking like black rice, at the main entrance.

Living under the snow has two main advantages. It provides protection against most predators and it can be up to 20°F. warmer there than at the surface, for snow is an excellent insulator. When the insulating value of the nest is added, the air temperature inside can reach 50°F., even when there is a heavy frost outside. In the tunnels, the lemmings' bodies press against the roofs and sides, packing the snow so closely in places that a thin shell will remain when the thaw sets in, showing where the burrow has led to the nest. I have also been able to trace the tunnels when the snow has melted away by lines of dead grass where the roots have been eaten. This litters the exposed floors of the tunnels like long, brown ropes.

Once the sun returns, the lemmings start to make short forays above the surface. It may be that changes in the consistency of the snow damage the tunnels, that the lemmings are seeking mates, or that they have eaten most of the food within easy reach. The birth of a litter will often aggravate a local food shortage. Having left their winter quarters, the adult lemmings will move nervously around, alert to predators.

Lemmings flourish only in the most favourable conditions and any great climatic change may cause death. Spring is a particularly perilous time, carrying with it the risk of flooding. Lemmings are also in danger at this time of year from the effects of a sudden frost after a thaw or shower of rain. Frost will glaze the herbage with ice, making grazing impossible and starvation almost inevitable.

But the greatest threat comes from predators. Throughout the year lemmings face a formidable range of enemies, for practically every claw and beak is against them. They are part of the diet of most large predators: among the mammals, bears, wolverines, martens, wolves, foxes, lynxes, weasels and stoats; among the birds, eagles, hawks, falcons, owls, skuas, gulls, ravens and occasionally magpies and shrikes.

Even in winter, when lemmings are living under the snow, there are still two enemies they really have to fear—the arctic fox and the stoat in its winter guise as ermine. The arctic fox stores lemmings in its food caches. It cannot follow the lemmings into their tunnels and so resorts to digging them out. In deep snow only about a third of its attempts may be successful. After sniffing out a lemming, the fox scrapes away some snow, jumps high in the air, as though launched from a trampoline, and lands back in the snow pit it has begun to dig. It will continue jumping until it has hollowed the snow sufficiently to scratch its way to its prey.

The stoat adopts less dramatic but equally successful tactics. It is slim and lithe enough to enter the tunnels in which lemmings live and will attack ferociously. Its hissing, whistling and squealing—similar, it has been said, to "a wet cork being rubbed on a bottle"—mingle for a while with its victim's own squeaks, but soon all is quiet. Stoats also are said to cache lemmings for food during the winter. I was told of one such cache that had been found in a hut and which also included mice, birds and frogs. There is a story that ermine and other beasts of prey eat ants during autumn and early winter to modify their urine for preserving their winter store. Most experts dismiss this, but I was told by my informant that he had noticed two distinct smells emanating from the cache: one of urine and another that resembled vinegar.

Danger from predators increases once the lemmings leave their snow tunnels, for the birds and beasts of prey will be seeking food for their females pregnant after the spring mating, and later for the newly-born young. Ravens, rough-legged buzzards, gulls and snowy owls are all quick to take lemmings at this time.

Reindeer are said to inflict a terrible revenge on lemmings for depriving them of so much of the lichen on which they depend. I heard of a Lapp who swore that in winter, when the reindeer are short of food, he had seen them tread the lemmings flat until they burst. The reindeer licked up the blood and fat of the lemmings, but left the flesh and skin, which were eagerly swooped on by ravens. I have also been told by Lapps that reindeer kill lemmings, not so much to eat the flesh or the fat as the undigested grass in their gut, and that it is for this reason they tread on the lemmings and squash them. Many reports, however, state that the flesh is also eaten.

Even in the water wandering lemmings are preyed on. Once, by a river I heard a squeal and saw a flurry among the ripples: a lemming had been seized by one of the trout for which Lapland is famous. The trout need not be huge. One weighing under four pounds had just swallowed a lemming when caught, and another fully grown lemming was being digested in its stomach. Salmon and grayling will take lemmings while they are swimming across rivers and a pike was once found to have eaten nine Norwegian lemmings and also two Forest lemmings, smaller relatives. Cod and other fish will attack lemmings in the sea.

Although lemmings invariably hesitate before entering deep water, either hopping up and down or running frantically backwards and forwards, they are able to swim quite well, propelling themselves with their hind legs. They have also been known to take advantage of favourable currents. Nevertheless, they drown in great numbers and I have seen scores of lemming corpses bobbing like brightly coloured rags on the waves. Lemmings are said to have keen eyesight, and one possible explanation for these drownings is that when they plunge into the water

A migrating Norwegian lemming leaves the safety of the shoreline and swims into the domain of such predatory fish as pike and trout.

they can see land in the offing—an island or the opposite shore of a fjord—not realizing how great the distance is.

In the face of so many hazards it is clear that lemmings must reproduce in great numbers to survive. Certainly, they have an extraordinary breeding capacity. The courtship begins charmingly, with the male sitting on his haunches near a receptive female, grooming his fur with sweeping movements of his forepaws, and the female imitating him. The mere odour of the female can set off so much male squealing that this sounds almost continuous. When the courtship pursuit begins, the female squeals too. At later stages there is less time for niceties. The male will chase any neighbour it imagines is a mateable female, and it has a powerful imagination, for it will court immature lemmings of either sex and even try to mate with a dead animal.

Females can conceive at a remarkably early age. In Finland some captive specimens provided amazing results in a year of abundance. One female's first litter arrived when she was only 35 days old. As the gestation period is some three weeks, she must have become pregnant at about 14 days, when she weighed not much more than half an ounce. Another female produced a first litter when 38 days old, so she had become pregnant at 17 days.

After conception the female builds a globular nest that she enlarges and repairs from inside after the young arrive. Litters, which contain more or less equal numbers of both sexes, follow at short intervals. The first litter may have no more than three young, but the second can have up to eight and the third up to ten. The females are almost continuously pregnant; for instance, a nest has been seen with eight large young ones of the third litter (some of them forced outside the nest) while at the bottom were six naked new-born young of the fourth set. In fact, it has been estimated that at the height of the population upswing, a single pair of lemmings could be responsible for hundreds, perhaps thousands, of descendants in one year.

All this refers to the long summer reproductive season, but it is now agreed that lemmings also breed in winter, at any rate in the first year of population increase, provided the conditions are neither too severe nor too mild (with dangerous thaws that lessen the snow cover and cause flooding). The babies, naked and blind, but able to squeak on the first day, weigh no more than a fraction of an ounce.

Many explanations have been advanced for the cyclic rises and falls in the numbers of lemmings. One popular theory a generation ago was that the cycles were linked in some way with the appearance of sunspots. Another theory, which is still given some currency from time to time, is that particularly powerful cosmic rays enhance the nutritional value of the herbage on which lemmings feed, thus increasing their fertility. Much controversy has also surrounded the suggestion that rises and falls in population are related to the amount of ozone in the atmosphere.

In fact, an upswing depends largely upon favourable weather conditions. An early spring and a late autumn will not only yield an abundance of food but allow the lemmings a longer period in which to take advantage of it. If the winter is not too prolonged and the spring of the following year not too cold, then an unusually high number of newly-born lemmings will survive, causing a population explosion.

But if the animals continued to reproduce at the rate of the peak years, the vegetation would be permanently damaged, food would become scarce and the very survival of the species threatened. When the population has reached a peak, therefore, breeding continues but, for reasons that are still unclear to naturalists, the young do not survive. At this stage, large numbers of lemmings may also leave the crowded habitats and set off on the famous migrations.

Some authorities object to the term "migration" because it implies an instinctive urge to seek out fresh territory, but even they accept that lemmings periodically wander in great numbers. What causes these mass wanderings? Spring floods will often drive adults from their winter quarters and many naturalists I have met also insist that food shortage is the main cause of migration. But overcrowding is certainly as important as flood or famine. Lemmings have an unsociable nature, barely tolerating one another at the best of times. As their numbers increase, so, too, does their restlessness. The adrenals of lemmings lack the reserve of fat that in an emergency helps to produce hormones in other animals. Lemmings are thus ill-equipped to bear stress and in peak years life in their habitats is tilted inexorably towards crisis.

A crowded habitat over an area of 100 square yards can contain more than 400 burrows. This density, and the strife that results, makes the lemmings almost demented; some move out, while others are driven out by those that are able to assert the most authority through their aggression. Since the original habitat is generally reckoned to be the most favourable, the advantage will lie with the lemmings that remain. They will have sufficient space and food and a large proportion of them will be young; others will be pregnant females and so the population can gradually increase in size.

But what about the displaced lemmings, those that wander off or are driven out? They do not move in family groups. At the start, one or two will stray from the habitat and others will gradually follow. But they do not behave like sheep, let alone soldiers on a route march. Some go off to one side or the other, a few wander in the opposite direction to the majority. Their numbers can be enormous and irregularly spaced out, and they tend to scuttle to and fro as they advance.

If the pressures that force them to wander are not too great, the lemmings seem to orientate themselves as soon as they set off, as though reacting to a light-compass. Such is the view of Professor Olavi Kalela, of Helsinki University, who observed migrations at Kilpisjärvi. When crossing the ice on the lake the lemmings were thought to be using the silhouette of Saana and other hills on the farther side as landmarks. They did not hold blindly to the orientation but took advantage of features such as ditches and banks for protection, avoiding steep slopes.

A vivid account was given to me of a lemming migration that took place one Easter nearly 50 years ago. My informant was preparing a log cabin for the holiday when he heard the sound of lemmings yelping. He went outside and peered out in the bright moonlight across the snow towards a long hill that sloped towards the cabin. Suddenly he noticed that the hill was carpeted with lemmings and that they were moving towards him. His Alsatian bitch sat petrified, waiting for the lemmings to arrive, and was stirred into action only when the first of them attacked. Some clung to her legs; others sat back on their haunches and tried to snap at the dog's nose. The dog then retaliated, striking the lemmings with her paws, taking the bodies in her mouth and tossing them high into the air. Several hundred were killed in this way before the dog retreated, but no noticeable gap was made in the "lemming carpet", which continued to unroll past the cabin.

I was told years ago that lemmings always migrate downhill, but the first time I saw Lapland lemmings on the move they were going uphill, back to the near-by Swedish fells they had left about three weeks before, at the beginning of May. They had probably shifted to better feeding grounds, less crowded, but were driven back by meltwater and were forced to seek dry ground higher up where appetizing vegetation was growing again. I saw numbers of them on the fells some days later.

W. Duppa Crotch, a Victorian traveller who wrote with charm about Norwegian lemmings, insisted that they always migrate westwards. According to him they were seeking Atlantis, where they had once discovered rich grazing, and persisted in heading for those pastures long sunk beneath the waves in which many lemmings perished. He thought that some had returned, thus maintaining the route. Naturalists are now convinced, however, that lemmings may migrate in any direction—upwards, downwards or horizontally, moving outwards from a central point, the original habitat.

Lemmings are no more companionable in water than they are on land, although they will sometimes plunge in together. Bunched up on the shore, their squabbles and fights will intensify and individuals may rush recklessly into the water, triggering off a mass swim by the whole party. Such incidents may have given rise to the idea that lemmings commit suicide by swimming out to death in the sea, fjords or lakes. Water—or any other obstacle that bars their way—may lead to mounting confusion and panic, but such suicidal surges are rare.

Not much is known about the exact distances lemmings cover. One report tells of a 280-mile journey from Finland into Russia, but this is quite exceptional, and the next longest migration I found recorded was of 87 miles, this time in the Kola peninsula. Other reports tell of journeys of only a few miles. A typical migration in Finland covered about ten miles in 24 hours.

I tried to establish just how many lemmings may be involved in mass wanderings. It is all very well to speak of armies, hordes and swarms, but I wanted precise figures. The details I came across at first seemed disappointing. A lemming every second, or 100 an hour, were two typical reports. Then I came across a report of six lemmings to the square yard in the region of Murmansk in 1930, and 300 lemmings, 80 shrews and about 100 field mice killed in a small field in Nordland in 1839 and—far to the south—one terrier killing 274 lemmings in an hour and a half.

According to Professor Kalela, of Helsinki University, not all the wandering lemmings necessarily die out. He believes that at least some of them survive to breed in new areas, thus extending the range of distribution as well as evening out differences in population density. If he is correct, then these wanderers have my lasting gratitude, for they will play a vital part in ensuring that one of the most captivating of Lapland species never dies out.

NATURE WALK / # In the Northern Wilderness

TEXT AND PHOTOGRAPHS BY TOBY MOLENAAR

The helicopter broke through the cloud ceiling without warning. Below was a primeval landscape of crags and peaks towering menacingly above snowfields and hanging glaciers. "Sarek Park," shouted our pilot, with a wave of his arm that embraced the whole horizon. I looked at the forbidding mountains again, and recalled the blunt warning I had read in the Swedish Tourist Guide: "People who have no experience in the Scandinavian mountain wilderness should stay away from Sarek National Park. It is no place for tourists."

Sarek Park was established by the Swedish government in 1909 to preserve an unspoiled mountain region together with its alpine flora and wildlife. The Park covers 750 square miles of Swedish Lapland just east of where the Kjölen mountain range forms a natural border with Norway. Within its boundaries is a magnificent world of snow-capped peaks and glaciated valleys, of streams and waterfalls that rush foaming down precipitous, forested slopes to meet the rivers and lakes below. It is regarded as the most inaccessible wilderness in western Europe. Few people live here; only the mountain Lapps have come to terms with the

Park's rugged terrain, the cold that grips it for all but a few summer months and the melancholy darkness that veils it during the long winter. Now, two of us—my guide, Tore, and myself, a photographer— were about to invade this inhospitable world.

Our pilot touched down at the northern tip of Lake Sitojaure, on the eastern fringe of the Park. He helped unload our rucksacks, and after telling us he would pick us up at the same point in three days' time, he took off. The helicopter climbed slowly, hovering for a second as though reluctant to abandon us to the mountains. Then it banked, the pilot waved farewell, and we watched the aircraft's winking red tail light vanish in the distance.

For a moment we gazed at our alien setting. We had left the small lumber-town of Gällivare an hour or two before in the bright autumnal sunshine of early October. Here, only 80 miles to the west, winter's grip had begun to tighten on the land. Swirls of snow drifted over rocks with a thin, rustling sound. Behind us the half-frozen lake surface reflected a leaden sky. On our left the snow-streaked flanks of Takartjåkkå rose almost sheer, its

5,000-foot summit hidden in clouds. A frozen stream threaded north towards a shallow glaciated valley. Along its stony course scruffy dwarf willows and clumps of arctic heath struggled through the snow. Frail blades of grass stood watch beside black splashes of open water.

Tore broke the silence by taking

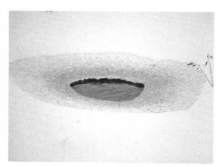

GRASS BY A HOLE IN THE ICE

out a map and showing me our route. We would follow the stream north for some miles along the Sitoätno valley until it forked west into the Pastavagge valley, which funnels deep into the mountains. This would take us right round the southern slopes of a 6,000-foot-high mountain, Äpartjåkkå, the pinnacle of the ice-capped Äpar massif, before it descends to Lake Pierikjaure. From the lake we would make a wide circle round the massif before rejoining the Sitoätno valley and returning to our rendezvous beside Lake Sitojaure.

Most of our route along Pastavagge lay between the tree-line and the permanent snow-line, in what is termed the montane zone. This is a world almost devoid of vegetation, stripped naked to reveal the bare

ICE-LOCKED SITOÄTNO STREAM

MALE REINDEER ISSUING A MATING CALL

bones of the earth. It is a zone of extremes and of paradox. Plants that grow in it must contend not only with winter's cold, snow and darkness but also survive the summer glare of ultra-violet radiation and the rapid fluctuations between day and night temperatures.

Harsh Conditions

They face alternate flooding and drought. They must seek footholds on solid rock, on moving scree slopes or on scanty pockets of acid soil. Few species have adapted to meet all these harsh conditions, but their very scarcity made me all the more eager to seek out and, if possible, photograph some of these hardy plants. We set off towards Pastavagge, our boots slipping on boulders hidden under clumps of heather and dwarf willow.

Our first encounter with Sarek's wildlife was unexpected. We rounded a bend and looked up to see a lone bull reindeer standing directly in our path, the colours of his glossy autumn coat blending with the patchwork landscape. The wind blew directly towards us and at first he was oblivious of our presence. He stood statuesquely still, the wind ruffling his pale mane; then he stretched out his neck, threw back his magnificently antlered head, and roared a throaty mating call across the valley. The click of my camera shutter betrayed us. The reindeer turned smoothly, and effortlessly bounded away up the valley.

While we stood looking after the retreating reindeer, the sun slid out from above a ledge of clouds, its wintry rays lending colour to a landscape that, until now, had possessed the stark quality of a photo-negative. The dull, brown heaths took on soft sable and purple tints, and tiny leaves of dwarf willow that I had barely noticed before made yellow and russet splashes against the snow. Where the sunlight touched frond-like growths of lichen, a pale green light seemed to glow from within the plant. On the marshy margins of the stream-bed, clumps of cotton-grass, each stem adorned with a nodding white beard, rippled in the wind. Grasses decked with drops of melted snow were transformed into strings of liquid light.

New Perspective

This gentler face of the wilderness showed itself only fleetingly before the sun was again swallowed up by clouds. When it had vanished, the plants seemed to withdraw into the rocks and the colours drained out of the valley. But I had seen enough to realize that if I wanted to explore Sarek's plant life I must adjust my perspective of nature. I must forget the profuse colours and tall trees of lowlands. Here, in the mountains, the plants grow low, forming creeping mats that escape the winds and exploit the comparatively warm layer of air that exists just above ground level. Their flowers are often small, for large blooms would be

BEARDED HEAD OF COTTON-GRASS

ripped to shreds by the wind.

We reached the mouth of Pastavagge in the late afternoon when darkness was already beginning to sift into the valley, and pitched camp on some flat ground dissected by a network of braided streams. While Tore put up the tents I stood looking into the gaping jaws of the valley

that we would climb next day. A strong wind played among rock buttresses with a booming sound and carried the distant clatter of falling scree. I shivered. As if sensing my thoughts, Tore looked up and said: "Pastavagge is the loneliest valley in Sarek. Even the Lapps avoid it. They say it is an unhappy place." I secretly agreed and wondered what it would look like in the depth of winter if now, in early October, it aroused in me this sense of foreboding.

Water was fetched from a stream, and because there was not a stick of wood for miles we heated up sweet fruit soup on a portable kerosene cooker. That night I sampled the food that would sustain us for the next few days: dried reindeer meat washed down by hot milky chocolate. Revived by this meal, we sat

FOLIOSE LICHEN CETRARIA NIVALIS

MELTED SNOW ON WOOD MILLET

SCREES AND MORAINE IN PASTAVAGGE

MUSHROOM ON MOSS CUSHION

watching night blot out the bulk of Äpartjåkkå to the west, until the cold drove us into our tents. The chill seeped into my sleeping bag, preventing sleep, and for a long time I lay listening to the changing song of the wind. It seemed to circle around my tent, rising on a higher-pitched note and falling to a strident wail that had a despairing human quality. Only much later did I learn that the Lapps call Äpartjåkkå the "mountain of the ghost of a murdered child".

During the night the wind died to a murmur, a thaw set in, and we awoke to find Pastavagge valley bathed in sunshine. Wispy clouds floated like steam from a witch's cauldron among rock spires and pinnacles. Above frost-shattered scree slopes and a glacial moraine that had been colonized by heaths, the fluted crests of the valley glinted like wet slate.

Complex Web

I went to fetch water from the stream, and discovered a small mushroom with melting ice crystals. The head of a mushroom is the fruiting body. I knew that in the thin soil beneath the moss was a complex web of fungal threads extracting nourishment from the soil by dissolving and absorbing organic materials.

We began our climb up Pastavagge valley, Tore leading. Above 2,500 feet the dwarf willows were at the limit of their endurance, growing barely above ankle height. Their place was largely taken by red-fruited cowberries, glossy, low-spreading

CREEPING AZALEA AND DWARF WILLOW

pink flowers of a creeping azalea.

Shortly after noon we crossed the watershed that divides Pastavagge and began our descent around the south-west shoulder of the Äpar massif towards Lake Pierikjaure. Äpartjäkkä reared skywards on our right. To our left, a débris-strewn glacier—one of 96 that lick down into Sarek's valleys — discharged streams of meltwater. The map indicated that we were at nearly 3,500 feet, and the change in altitude was reflected by a drop in temperature and the sparseness of the surrounding vegetation. Gone were the willows, the junipers and the creeping arctic shrubs. They were succeeded by a mat of woolly hair-moss and a greenish-grey lichen, *Cetraria islandica*. Their footing among the rocks

evergreen shrubs whose leathery leaves help reduce water-loss to a minimum. Like most of Sarek's 400 species of vascular plants, the cowberry's survival is not wholly reliant on a single method of reproduction. When summer temperatures are too low to ensure the successful germination of seeds, the species can produce underground runners that give rise to vegetable offspring.

Above the carpet of cowberry, on a rock face so steep that it lacked soil cover, a stunted fruiting juniper defied gravity, its tortuous roots straggling across bare rock to find support and nutrition in the few shallow fissures where soil had formed. Below the rock, in a cranny sheltered from the wind, bright yellow leaves of dwarf willow framed the tiny

FRUITING COWBERRY

FRUITING JUNIPER

was tenuous: in places the moss and lichen carpet had been ripped up by the wind. But on the wind-bared rocks, scattered growths of younger plants showed that the slow process of colonization had begun again.

To our surprise, the lower we descended and the nearer we got to Lake Pierikjaure, the colder the air grew. When we rounded the western shoulder of the massif the change of weather was even more marked. Thick mist rolled down the amphi-theatre of the lake towards water that had a cold grey hue, imparted by glacial sediments.

On the lake shore, spiky tufts of

SNOW-CAPPED GRASS TUSSOCK

grass, looking like hedgehogs, broke through the snow, their compact growth and layers of dead leaves effectively combating the heat- and moisture-sapping effects of the wind. The marked transition from the snow-free eastern half of Pastavagge

to the wintry panorama around the lake, reminded me that mountains make their own climate. Temperatures can plunge in seconds as a downdraught sweeps cold air from ice-capped summits. In fact, parts of the high peaks may be warmer than valleys, following a clear, frosty night when frozen ground chills a layer of air that settles in the valleys. On a sunny slope a patch of soil that is sheltered from the wind may be $40°$ F. warmer than a less well-situated patch only a few yards distant. In the mountains there are climates within climates.

We walked down to the lake, skirt-

STEELY-GREY LAKE PIERIKJAURE

ing heaps of glacial débris crowned by the yellow-tipped, lance-like leaves of fir clubmoss. I examined one of the mosses more closely and saw that miniature counterparts of the adult plant grew in its leaf axils. When I touched one of these plant-lets it broke off, and I realized that it was a vegetative offshoot, easily de-tached by the wind and capable of developing into a mature plant.

We brewed tea by the lake and discussed where we would camp that night. Conversation was inter-rupted by the sight of two reindeer— a bull in hot pursuit of a cow— making towards us. The cow saw us

REINDEER PAIR CROSSING THE LAKE

FIR CLUBMOSS

first and, with hardly a pause, swung round and plunged into the icy lake, her would-be mate hard on her heels. Together they swam powerfully through the choppy water towards the opposite shore, almost a mile away. In about a month's time, when the rutting season was over, this pair would rejoin the herd. Then, as winter blizzards buried the lichen pastures in the mountains, the rein-deer would move slowly down the valleys to the forest where they would scrape a diet of lichens

and grasses from beneath the snow.

We camped at the northern tip of the lake, and started out early next morning, heading back to Lake Sito-jaure and our rendezvous with the helicopter. Fresh snow had fallen overnight, drifting so deep in places that only the long stems of grasses broke through its surface. About mid-morning a dense mist descended, obscuring the mountains and mak-ing navigation by compass neces-sary. We slogged blindly over the broken terrain, getting colder and wetter as the mist laid its clammy hand upon us. From time to time we heard an eerie croaking issuing from the rocks around us, but it was not until a covey of ptarmigan, already resplendent in winter-white plum-age, burst up from our path that we recognized the source of the sound. Farther on, Tore came across the clean-picked carcass of one of these mountain grouse, and pointed out

wedge-shaped bites in its breastbone, the work, he said, of a gyr falcon.

When we reached Lake Sitojaure just after noon, the helicopter was waiting. Its pilot, seeing us shamble out of the mist towards him, our faces burned and eyes reddened by three days' exposure to sun and wind, must have imagined we looked like survivors of a shipwreck. The thought of an immediate return to civilization was enticing. But I had decided that morning to prolong my

GRASSES AMID SNOW

stay in Sarek and explore its less austere world of forests. Tore had told me of an old Lapp couple with whom I could stay at their home on Lake Laitaure, just outside the Park's eastern border, only ten miles from the Äpar Massif. An hour later the helicopter put me down by the lake shore, and I watched the machine rise into the sky and disappear.

Winter had come to the mountains, but around the lake autumn colours still glowed like the embers of a dying fire. The sun shone; pines grew thick at the water's edge, and from them came the excited chatter of small birds. Parties of crested tits flickered through the leaf canopy, briefly perching on boughs to forage for insect larvae in crevices in the bark. On a birch sapling I saw a

ANGELICA, A FAVOURITE OF BEARS

bronze-plumaged female pine grosbeak, its disproportionately massive bill an efficient tool for extracting seeds from rowan berries, a favourite food of the species.

I walked up through the pine forest. Above 1,500 feet the conifers grew smaller and at this altitude their limbs were contorted as if in

agony. Gaps appeared in their ranks and were filled by silver and russet birches and the blood-red leaves of rowans. In a moist, grassy glade grew the tall stems of angelica, their multi-branched heads now bare of flowers. Angelica is a delicacy reputed to be favoured by the brown bear, an animal that together with the lynx, elk, wolverine and, until recently, the wolf, finds a safe refuge in the Park. I found marks on a pine tree where a bear had scratched its claws. At this time of the year the bears would be foraging far and wide for food, greedily devouring everything from slugs to carrion, building up the layer of subcutaneous fat that would sustain them through their long winter hibernation.

I climbed higher. The pine forest petered out. Above me a grove of birches still bearing some of their leaves made a last stand before giving way to dwarf willows. Sunlight slanted through the trees, fracturing in dapples against their silver trunks and highlighting clusters of red berries that hung from the branches of a few rowans.

Scolding chatter

I sat at the foot of a birch and looked at the mountains reflected in the lake below. It was quiet here, but without the oppressive stillness of the mountains. A hidden stream tinkled among the rocks. Somewhere a hooded crow called raucously and was answered by the scolding chatter of a red squirrel. A vole rustled urgently across the dry leaf carpet, driven by the imminent approach of winter to swell its larder of berries

FEMALE PINE GROSBEAK

SUNLIT SILVER BIRCHES

and nuts before deep snow cut off its food supplies.

The next day was my last in Sarek. Sigurd, my Lapp host, suggested that a fitting climax to my visit would be a journey to the Laitaure delta at the head of the lake, and he offered to guide me through the forest. Sigurd had a fierce, almost proprietary love of his wilderness home, knew every inch of it, and was an excellent and willing teacher. He showed me black beard lichens that festooned the branches of pines, and told me that these were what reindeer are forced to eat during unusually severe winters, when a hard crust of ice forms on the ground, sealing off the grasses and lichens beneath.

Pausing under a tall pine surrounded by compact pellets of feathers

ROWAN BERRIES

and bones, he pointed out an untidy nest about 50 feet up in which three goshawks had been raised that year.

A deadly predator, with long, sickle-like claws, the goshawk impressed even Attila with its fierceness and was used by "the Scourge of God" as a personal emblem. Yet, the goshawk leads an irreproachable family life. During incubation the female is provided with food by her mate, and after the young have been hatched the male delivers food to the whole family. The female takes the prey from the male, tearing it into shreds and offering the pieces to the chicks. Not until the chicks are almost full-grown does the female join in the search for food.

Throughout the walk Sigurd held my rapt attention. It seemed no time before we emerged from the shade of the forest to see the convoluted form of the delta spread out below a black and white backdrop of snow-streaked mountains. Looping towards the apex of the delta was the river Rapaätno, swollen by melt-water and loaded with débris from some 30 or so glaciers that lie above its course. Each year the river dumps more than 100,000 tons of sediment at the head of Lake Laitaure, and each year currents carve new channels in the silt, washing it away in places, depositing it in others, thus creating ever-changing patterns within the delta.

Precarious Foothold

Willows and alders, pioneering trees that can colonize waterlogged habitats denied to other species, grew in a thick curtain around the delta, drawing nutrition from the comparatively fertile silt and helping to bind the uncompacted glacial sediments. Their foothold on the shifting banks was precarious; in many places spring floods had uprooted them, and now they sprawled half-submerged in the water, moss-covered roots groping blindly above the surface.

Behind the delta were acres of bogland colonized by sedges and horse-tails. From an evolutionary point of view, horsetails have not come very far since they made their début among the world's flora more than 300 million years ago. At that time, these early ancestors of present-day ferns were among the dominant plant species, growing to heights of more than 40 feet and covering vast tracts

of tropical land in dense, steamy forests. The horsetails growing around the delta were no higher than one foot, but their shape and primitive method of reproduction—by means of microscopic spores produced in sacs on their leaves—are identical with those of their far-off ancestors.

The labyrinthine maze of the delta is a paradise for waders and water-fowl, Sigurd said, but most species had already migrated south. I scanned the sky and saw a fast-moving white speck flying arrow-straight down the middle of the lake. As it passed us I caught a faint, son-orous bugling note, the call of a whooper swan. Only one or two pairs actually breed in the delta, Sigurd explained. They use it every year as a marshalling zone before and after their spring and autumn migrations.

We left the delta and climbed Skierfe, one of the three peaks that guard the head of the lake. At the summit we looked back. From this height the delta's network of channels and lagoons looked as though they had been created by a child drawing its fingers across a paint palette, mixing soft colours in an abstract pattern of sinuous lines. Behind the delta reared the bulk of Nammatj, isolated from its neighbours by two valleys, one each side, that had been cut by glaciers. Pink clouds floated motionless in the sky. Two rough-legged buzzards sailed past on splay-tipped wings, mewing plaintively to each other. They found a thermal rising off the shady forest, and we watched them soar effortlessly up into the darkening sky.

NAMMATJ AND LAKE LAITAURE

5/ Lake, Rivers and Forest

Some of the old pines, scathed and branchless, stand like spectres among their living brethren; while others, borne down by old age, lie rotting in the wind and sun.

H. W. WHEELWRIGHT/ *A SPRING AND SUMMER IN LAPLAND*

It was a very hot day. Above me, the crest of the fell I was climbing shimmered in a heat haze; swarms of biting insects nevertheless forced me to put on the hood of my anorak, adding to the discomfort of a throat parched by long slogging across rocks and tussocks. For the hundredth time since arriving in Lapland, I wondered at the perverseness of a climate that so far north produces temperatures that would do justice to some Mediterranean resort. Rounding a boulder that guarded the crest of the fell, however, I immediately forgot the heat, the insects and my aching leg muscles. Below me was an immense panorama of Finnish Lapland, a wilderness of lakes, rivers and forest.

Dominating the landscape was Lake Inari, 50 miles long and 25 miles wide, the largest body of fresh water in Lapland. From my vantage point high above Inari's southern coastline I scanned the wilderness in vain for the road I had followed from the town of Kirkenes, one hundred miles to the north. In front of me the blue waters of the lake, offset by the green of countless islands, vanished over the curve of the northern horizon. Eastwards they met a low range of forested hills, studded with lakes and dissected by rivers, that extended beyond the Soviet border, only 20 miles distant.

I had come here, to this remote north-eastern corner of Finnish Lapland, to explore what is, in effect, a meeting place of several worlds. It is a sort of amphibious region, neither land nor water but a mosaic of both, a confused pattern of lakes and streams separated by belts of forest, bog and bare fells. In one respect, its landscape is younger than the rest of Lapland. For while the uplands to the west were moulded largely by the advance of the glaciers of the last Ice Age, eastern Lapland owes its surface features to the retreat of the ice—a process that came to an end only some 10,000 years ago.

Here, on the relatively flat foundations of the Baltic Shield, an area of ancient, worn-down and stable rocks that extends east from the Scandinavian mountain chain into Russia, the advancing glaciers met almost no resistance. Grinding steadily over the region, they left little more than broad, shallow depressions in their wake. When the ice sheet melted, however, it deposited its load of eroded material, burying much of the bare rock with boulder clay, choking up former river valleys—thus radically altering the region's pre-glacial drainage system—and damming up the ice-gouged depressions. These depressions subsequently filled with melt-water and much of the land was inundated by a bewildering network of lakes.

Besides being a meeting point for land and water, eastern Lapland is a transition zone as regards climate: here, far from the damp and relatively mild winds of the Atlantic, the continental-type climate characteristic of Siberia begins to assert itself. As one moves eastwards, the summers become shorter and more parched, the winters longer and more cold. The shift is marked by a change in vegetation, for east of Inari the scattered coniferous forests merge with the conifers and birches of the biggest forest on earth—the taiga—which marches all the way across northern Asia to the shores of the Pacific. I decided, therefore, that after exploring the Inari region I would head roughly north from the lake down the Pasvik valley, which holds the most westerly offshoot of the taiga.

Wolverines and bears, which have all but disappeared from most parts of Lapland, are permanent if rarely seen residents in Pasvik, while elk are more numerous there than elsewhere in the region. The deep forest harbours the great grey owl, a bird so rare in Scandinavia that virtually nothing is known of its habits. There have also been sightings of the Siberian nutcracker and the white-winged crossbill, species that occur in the rest of Lapland only in irruption years, when over-population forces them out from their taiga strongholds to the east.

During my descent from the fell towards Inari's southern shore I became so engrossed in my forthcoming journey that I disregarded ominous dark clouds building up over the lake. By the time I was halfway

124/

down the fell, thunder reverberated, lightning flared across the sky and heavy drops of rain stippled the lake surface. Then, slowly, the storm moved westwards and the thunder died away in the distance. As I reached the shore the sun emerged again and a brilliant rainbow arched across the glittering water.

I was standing on the banks of a sheltered inlet, one of the hundreds that bite into Inari's shore line. On each side the silvery trunks of birches gleamed against a dark green backdrop of pines, while a fringe of trailing willow branches formed dense trellis-work on the lake margins. Close to the water's edge, many of the trees sprawled at crazy angles, victims of the turbulence caused by spring and autumn storms. Now, however, the lake surface was calm, the water so clear that I could detect the bleached skeleton of a shrub lying 15 feet below the surface. Close inshore, where the water was calmest, I saw minute black insects gyrating upon the surface film. They were whirligig beetles, winged insects that feed on dead or disabled land animals trapped on the surface film of water. In their search for food, the whirligigs can fly readily from one stretch of water to another, and if disturbed while resting or feeding, they dive beneath the surface, carrying with them a personal oxygen supply in the form of a small air-bubble.

Below the water was a world of truly aquatic organisms, some vegetable, some animal. A shoal of young minnows, their bodies flashing in the sunlight, swam into view, darting first in one direction, then another. I surmised that their erratic movements were due to localized groupings of plankton—microscopic plants on which the minnows were feeding. As the tiny fish finished cropping one small area of plankton, they moved to another, perhaps only a few inches away.

While plankton form a major food supply for free-swimming predators, countless millions of these minute organisms die a natural death and drift slowly to the bed of the lake, where their remains are devoured by sedentary bottom-dwelling creatures. One of these scavengers was just visible through several feet of unclouded water. Half buried among the pebbles was a pea-mussel, a small bivalve mollusc that has rows of minute, hairlike cilia on its gills. By perpetually waving its cilia, the pea-mussel stirs a faint current of water over and through its gills, trapping plankton and decayed organic matter.

Worms, insect larvae and small crustaceans also live a precarious existence on the lake-bed, although they prefer the richer feeding to be had where there is mud cover on the floor. Such a place existed farther along the inlet, and there the struggle for survival, although small in

Huddled close to the trunk of a birch tree in a forest at Varanger, Norwegian Lapland, an immature great grey owl waits for its parents to bring it food. At this time of year, early summer, it probably will not have to wait long, because food is usually plentiful.

scale, could be ferocious. I had not long to wait. As my eyes adjusted to this new perspective of the wilderness, I saw a pale brown insect swimming underwater with powerful strokes of its long, hair-fringed, segmented legs. It was a waterboatman, one of the fiercest insect predators, which kills and eats fish and insects up to three times its size. As I watched, the waterboatman changed direction and, swimming with a rapid sculling motion, swam to the bottom of the lake, where its arrival caused a caddis fly larva to vanish abruptly into its home-made "shell" of twigs and pebbles. Frustrated, the waterboatman swam off and disappeared to forage in a patch of weeds.

So far, the only fish I had seen were minnows, but a sudden splash about 20 yards away indicated that something bigger was on the move. Looking up, I saw small ripples spreading outwards in concentric rings near the opposite side of the inlet, just under some overhanging alder trees. Another set of ripples appeared, then another, and within seconds the whole surface under the trees was ruffled. Then, as abruptly as it had begun, the activity slackened and the lake was as calm as before. I realized that I had just seen a series of what fishermen call rises. Aquatic insects, probably alder fly larvae, which had spent up to two years on the lake floor, had risen to the surface to shed their skins for the last time and to embark on their brief lives as flying insects. The swirls of water, or rises, suggested that feeding fish darting to the surface had cut short many of the flies' new-found freedom.

The feeding fish were almost certainly trout, which are numerous in virtually all Lapland lakes, rivers and streams. Inshore at Inari typical mature specimens weigh about two pounds and feed principally on minnows and small crustaceans, as well as on hatching insects. Farther out, in deep water, lurk the cannibal trout, hook-jawed monsters that sustain their bulk of 20 pounds or more with a diet of smaller fish. Although so different in appearance and feeding habits, both types of trout belong to the same species, *Salmo trutta*. Nor are they the only variations of the species to be found in Lapland. At different times of the year, Inari, with its wide range of habitats, supports the sedentary brown trout, the migratory sea-trout, and the lake trout, which spends part of its life in rivers and part in lakes.

Although trout thrive in the pure, well-oxygenated waters of Inari, they face competition from a more typical arctic species, the yellow-spotted, red-bellied char. The two species co-exist uneasily in the same habitats, the trout usually dominating in lowland waters, the char dominating in the high alpine zone. Like salmon, most char spend the

Buoyed up by air trapped beneath its wing cases and among the tiny hairs that grow on its abdomen, an aptly-named waterboatman rests against the underside of the surface film. The waterboatman's buoyancy is not so helpful when the insect feeds on the bottom of a lake. It has to swim constantly downwards, or anchor itself on to a twig or pebble, to keep from being carried back to the surface.

128/

greater part of their lives in the sea, returning to the rivers and lakes only to spawn. Many populations, however, are non-migratory and spend their whole lives in fresh water, sometimes in land-locked lakes. Perhaps these fresh-water char have evolved from their migratory relatives, but a more interesting theory is that they were introduced into the lakes by Lapp reindeer herders, as a living food supply for their seasonal trek to the coast.

It is no accident that the highly-prized species in Lapland are all game fish belonging to the *Salmonidae* family. Many so-called coarse fish, such as tench and carp, are too sluggish to survive in the fast-flowing rivers, while the lakes, ice-bound and deprived of sunlight for much of the year, are poor in the vegetation on which these fish feed. The coarse species that have adapted to the harsh environment are all carnivorous. The pike, a gaunt, wolf-mouthed killer that haunts the reedy fringes of Inari, lies in wait for such species as roach and perch. The handsomely striped perch preys on the shoals of silvery bleak that swarm in the shallows, and the bleak, in turn, make inroads on the water insects.

By now I had explored the inlet and was beginning to make my way round the southern edge of the lake, towards the Ivalo, Inari's chief tributary river. At first I followed a narrow gravel beach strewn with twigs and other odds and ends of débris washed up by the water. But soon I was forced to struggle over lichen-covered rocks and claw my way through dense birch scrub. There were diversions: emerging suddenly from a thicket I surprised a raven that took to the air with a guttural call of protest, leaving behind the remains of an eel on which it had been gorging. The eel could well have been killed by an otter, for although this elusive mammal takes trout and salmon, its favourite prey also appears to include eel. But in winter, when the eels hibernate beneath the mud and the lakes are frozen over, the otter is forced down to the coast, where it hunts the estuaries and bays for shellfish.

Farther on, the birch trees grew so thick near the water's edge that I was compelled to strike inland. Away from the boggy lake margins, the birches gave way to conifers and soon I was breathing the warm, scented air of a pine forest. For almost an hour I walked in a deep silence. No birds called, no insects whirred, and my footsteps were muffled by a thick carpet of pine needles. Then, ahead of me, I heard the sound of running water. Through gaps in the trees I caught glimpses of a swirling river and suddenly I emerged from the forest on to the banks of the Ivalo.

At this point, about one hundred miles from its source in the fells on the Norwegian-Finnish border, the Ivalo runs through a cutting rimmed

Mouth agape, a predatory pike holds a three-spined stickleback in its jaws. The pike, the most voracious of Europe's freshwater fish, is armed with two arsenals of teeth. The large, almost straight teeth in the lower jaw serve to wound its prey, and then the mass of backward-pointing teeth in the palate guide the disabled victim into the pike's throat.

with pale cliffs before broadening out and disgorging into the southern-most tip of Inari. Upstream, in the direction I was heading, it meanders through the pine forest. The river was low now, and smooth boulders broke its surface, but I could see where, swollen by spring melt-water, it had flooded the banks on each side of its course, scouring away the vegetation and cutting channels through the necks of the meanders.

Drowsy from my journey through the forest, I paused to rest for a moment on a stone slab overlooking a stretch of rapids. Lulled by the sound of swirling water and by the warmth of the afternoon sun, I was half dozing when my attention was caught by a fish that leapt from an eddy almost directly below. I glimpsed only a steel-grey back, sequined with scales, and a sail-like dorsal fin, but that was enough for me to identify it as a grayling. To me this fish, which occurs only in the purest lakes and rivers, embodies the spirit of Lapland waters. Others do not share my admiration, maintaining that the grayling destroys large quantities of valuable salmon eggs and fry, and that the flesh, although delicately tasting of thyme when fresh, deteriorates all too rapidly.

According to Izaak Walton, the father of freshwater angling, the grayling feeds on gold. His supposition was not quite as absurd as it sounds, for the typical grayling habitat of fast-flowing, gravelly streams sometimes carries alluvial deposits of the precious metal. The Ivalo is such a stream, and in spite of its remoteness it did not escape the gold fever that swept much of the world in the 19th Century. Hopeful prospectors struggled into the valley to seek their fortunes, but few realized their dreams and, penniless and disillusioned, they soon drifted back to the cities. Elsewhere they were luckier. For instance at Laanila, south of Inari, a prospector found a nugget weighing nearly 14 pounds.

Relics of the Lapland goldrush can still be found along the Ivalo. Farther upstream, at a place where the river flows through a patch of meadowland, I came across a dilapidated row of sluice boxes, used for separating the heavy gold particles from the lighter river gravel. Piles of worked-over gravel lay by the riverside and I amused myself by sorting through one, half hoping to find a small particle of gold. Almost immediately, I caught a glimpse of metal. Scarcely believing my luck, I unearthed a tiny, shining yellow granule. But somehow the "gold" did not seem right; it was too yellow, and when I scraped it with a fingernail, it flaked easily. My excitement died as I realized that I was holding nothing more valuable than a particle of ferrous sulphide—fool's gold. It was time, I decided, for me to head back to Inari.

Early next day I began to explore one of the lake's main outlets. Called the Paats where it drains out of the eastern shore of Lake Inari, this river courses for a short way through Finland and then cuts across a slice of the U.S.S.R. before entering northern Norway. Thereafter it is called the Pasvik and flows about 60 miles along the Norwegian-Russian border, before entering Varangerfjord, near Kirkenes.

Compared to the Alta and the Tana, the two great arteries to the west that drain the vidda, the Pasvik is neither large nor spectacular. What most sets it apart from the other rivers of Lapland is the taiga-type landscape that skirts it early on its course through Norway. In order to preserve this unique habitat, part of the upper reaches of the Pasvik valley, a flat, low-lying area broken up by small lakes, has been designated a National Park. It was near here that I spent the night.

Next morning I dressed and breakfasted hurriedly, impatient to reconnoitre the taiga. But it was with an increasing sense of foreboding that I left the river and headed into the primeval forest. I was experiencing the civilized man's fear of a world where distance and direction have no meaning. I saw sinister significance in the incomprehensible gestures of the pines, some of them tortured into fantastic shapes, which alternated with straggling birch stands and pools of stagnant water. In places, vivid green patches fringed with willow warned me of bogs, while farther on the trees gave way to small heath-like areas with wiry heather and creeping bilberry. Several times I came across clearings that were completely bare of vegetation and piled with rocks—ideal sites, it seemed, for heathen rites.

Within minutes I was hopelessly lost. My map of the region turned out to be inaccurate and the compass could not warn me of any hazards that lay ahead. So I followed a stream, hoping that it would lead me to a river or lake where I could get my bearings. For what seemed an hour I trudged the obstacle course of the stream, until it abruptly terminated in a bog. Nor was my erratic progress helped by the confused nature of the terrain, for although the region is undeniably flat, it is broken up by random lines of low ridges and mounds interspersed with depressions and shallow, blind valleys from which surface water cannot escape.

The taiga here is so flat that surface water does not possess enough erosive force to cut deep, well-defined channels as it does in more hilly regions. Each spring, when the winter snowfall melts, the land is flooded. The floodwater drowns trees, creates new streams, and alters existing courses. When viewed from the air, the endless rolling billows of conifers and birches may look solid and permanent enough, but here,

Lake Inari, shown freezing up during an autumn snow shower, is the largest lake in Lapland. Within its area of over 400 square miles are some 3,000 islands of varying size that are thickly covered with birch, pine and spruce trees. Its freshwaters are rich with life—ranging from microscopic plankton to large, aggressive cannibal trout and pike.

on the ground, I could see that the taiga is in a state of constant change.

The heavy scent of pine resin led me presently to a belt of trees that had been overrun by fire. On the fringes of this blackened area some pines that had survived the flames, although badly scorched, carried colonies of bracket fungi on their trunks. The fungi had gained a foothold on the trees through wounds inflicted by the fire, and now they were feeding on their hosts, dooming the trees to rot and die.

Some trees, already decaying, bore scars inflicted by woodpeckers that had been attracted to the insects living in the dead wood. They could have been made by any one of four species that live in the Pasvik taiga: the black, the great spotted, the lesser spotted and the three-toed woodpecker. The three-toed species is typical of the taiga, being more common to the east of the Lapland border, but from the size of the holes I guessed that they had been excavated by the largest of them, the black woodpecker. Both species share a habit peculiar to Eurasian woodpeckers: they drill holes through pine and fir bark so as to drink the sap beneath. Sometimes they can be seen, motionless, their beaks buried in the liquid, and because the sap also attracts insects, the woodpeckers pick them up as a bonus.

Although I heard one drumming in the distance, I did not see any woodpeckers but I did find a family group of waxwings which, with their brown crests, yellow-tipped tails and red wing spots (like blobs of sealing wax) are among the most conspicuous of taiga birds. Waxwing populations fluctuate according to the supply of berries on which they feed, and in years when a rich crop of berries produces a population explosion, the waxwings irrupt westwards from their taiga stronghold. Some years they even cross the North Sea in large numbers and can be seen feeding on ornamental shrubs in city parks to the south and west—a sight that provokes dozens of calls to newspapers reporting flocks of "parrots" in London, Amsterdam or Berlin.

Time passed. I was beginning to think that I would spend the rest of my life wandering this wilderness when I came to a long, narrow, winding ridge, about 20 feet high. From a distance it looked remarkably like a railway embankment, and offered easier going on its crest. This ridge was an esker, a deposit of gravel laid down by a stream running under the ice sheet that once covered this region. On its comparatively well-drained slopes, pine trees grew in profusion, and in those places where flooding had washed away the soil between their roots, I noticed a pronounced example of soil banding.

At the surface was a thin, uncompacted layer of dark, acid humus, composed of the rotted remains of pine needles and other vegetation. Below this was a bleached, grey layer from which iron hydroxides had been leached into the next layer, a dark brown zone with the consistency of hardpan. This distinctive soil profile, called a *podzol*, is one of the characteristic soils of the taiga and is formed in cool climates where precipitation exceeds evaporation, causing certain surface minerals to be washed down to lower zones.

The esker gently lost height until it petered out in a marshy area on the margins of a small lake, which to my relief gave me my bearings at last. Deserting the higher, drier ground, I pushed my way down through cloudberry bushes and reached the muddy, sedge-strewn lake shore. Here I rested under the shade of a birch. Close by, a bluethroat, called the Swedish nightingale by Linnaeus, sang its repetitive but melodious call-note, and at the top of a willow I saw its eyecatching blue bib, marked with a red centre. Aware of me, the bluethroat promptly flew off deeper into the forest, granting me a glimpse of the rufous base of its tail.

The lake was smaller than Inari, but supported much richer vegetation. On bare mud between the sedges, I recognized the small, pinkish flowers of water purslane and the bright yellow petals of greater spearwort. Farther out was a plant that possesses no roots, the greater bladderwort. It lives a free-floating life, buoyed up by tiny bladders on its leaves.

Suddenly I heard the raucous alarm call of a hooded crow on the opposite shore of the lake. Looking up I saw a much larger bird flapping towards me above the tree tops. As it reached the lake it went into a glide and I recognized the sharply angled wings of an osprey. For a second I thought it would pass over my head, but then it veered off and commenced a slow, stately patrol of the lake, flying about 50 feet above the surface and scanning the water with quick movements of the head.

The osprey seemed to concentrate its attention on a stretch of shallow water next to a bed of sedges; and after making several passes over this area it paused in flight, hovered clumsily for a second, then plunged, wings folded and legs outstretched, towards the water, hitting it in a welter of spray. Moments later it re-emerged, flying ponderously, weighed down by a struggling fish clutched by its feet. Slowly the osprey gained height and I watched it shift its grip on the fish so that the prey pointed head foremost, reducing wind resistance. As the osprey reached the shore a pair of crows flew up from the trees to attack it and, calling noisily, harried it out of sight.

It was time to press on, so once more I braved the bogs and confusing

Dependent upon berries during Lapland's hard winter months, a waxwing perches on a source of supply: a branch of a guelder rose bush.

ridges of the taiga, heading on a line that would bring me back to the river Pasvik. I slept soundly in a deserted hut shared with numbers of insects which, instead of bothering me, spent their time bumping against a window pane trying to get out into the night-long sunshine.

The following day I moved farther downriver. For the first mile or two I walked in sight of a broad, slow-flowing reach that was dotted with reedy islands and choked in places by long fronds of waterweed. In the inlets that etched the bank I surprised shoals of young pike, called "jacks", lying in water so shallow that it barely covered them. At this stage of growth the pike feed on insects and fry of their own kind, but within a year they move into deeper water where they start to eat fish, a diet supplemented by water shrew and duckling.

From the reed-beds I could hear the clucking of water fowl as they chivvied their half-fledged young, trying to keep them together, and I watched a family of bean geese strutting close into the shore, their dark grey heads moving in unison. Soon the adult males of many species would lose all their flight feathers, a type of moult known among ornithologists as eclipse, and then, within a few weeks, grow a new set for their autumn journey to the south. During the vulnerable period of flightlessness the birds try to avoid predators by confining themselves to the densest reed-beds.

Thus far there had been only an infrequent gurgle from the current, but now ahead of me it began to chatter, and rounding a bend I saw a stretch of broken water before the river bed changed to gravel. This gravel reach stirred memories of a similar section of river in southern Norway where I had seen two young girls diving for freshwater pearl mussels. At one time, pearls were also an important part of the economy of the Skolt Lapps who used the Pasvik valley as a migration route for their reindeer and owned fishing rights along the river. These Skolt Lapps were devout followers of the Russian Orthodox sect of the Christian faith—so devout, in fact, that a proportion of the pearls they found were sent to Russia for the adornment of clerical vestments.

I scanned the river bed hoping to see the smooth black outline of a mussel half buried in the gravel. None showed, but I was not too disappointed as I knew that the odds against my finding a mussel that contained a valuable pearl were hundreds, possibly thousands, to one. Before a pearl can form, a foreign body must enter the mussel causing irritation and loosening cells of nacre, or mother-of-pearl, which often line the shell. At one time it was thought that particles of sand stimulated pearl formation, but in river mussels the stimulus is usually provided by a larval parasite that lives for part of its life in swans and tufted ducks, the latter very common along the Pasvik.

Leaving the gravel reach behind, I followed a well-worn track that skirted the river. Although overgrown in parts, the track was clearly defined and I presumed that it had been worn down by Skolt Lapps making their seasonal journeys down to their camping grounds on the shores of Varangerfjord. Yet even these relatively primitive people were not the first to use the Pasvik valley as a migration route; they were following a trail that had been blazed by Stone Age hunters and fishermen thousands of years before. The progress of these prehistoric nomads is known from archaeological relics that have been discovered in the Pasvik valley. Axes and picks made from a greenish stone said to be found only far to the south near Rovaniemi, in Finland, hint that the trail-blazers had their origins south of the Arctic Circle.

Some distance farther on there was another sign that I was treading in the footsteps of earlier travellers. At one place along the track were a score of Siberian firs, their pale yellow-green foliage contrasting markedly with the darker needles of the pines. I was puzzled by their presence here because I knew that these trees do not normally occur in western Europe, but are, in fact, the species typical of the taiga east of the White Sea. Pondering on how these aliens had reached the Pasvik valley, I wondered whether, like the freshwater char in Lake Inari, they may have been introduced by the Skolt Lapps.

Other legacies of these migrations are the place names that the Lapps gave to key landmarks along the Pasvik valley. The Skolt Lapps no longer make the trek across the Soviet Union's border, but many names survive to conjure up visions of their ancient way of life. Lake Vaggatem, formed where the Pasvik widens and is swollen by streams entering it from the west, and towards which I now headed, is such a place. The Lapps refer to it as "the place where reindeer can break into a trot" for it was here that the reindeer herds, wearied by their hard slog through deep snow, could move on to Vaggatem's snow-covered ice and run the five-mile length of the lake.

After several hours of walking, I came in sight of the lake, blue as a new pair of jeans among the pines and birches. I walked westwards for a mile, skirting the rim of the lake, to where a long arm of water probed deep into the forest. Here, by the shore, I set up camp and, after a simple meal, wandered down to the water's edge. I could hear the reassuring gabbling of ducks and from far out there were the occasional plops of fish rising. The fluting whistle of a whimbrel sounded from the opposite shore and was answered by the eerie cry of a black-throated diver. These were the sounds of Lake Vaggatem in summer, and it was difficult on that warm, bright evening to imagine the lake as the Skolt Lapps must have seen it—on a winter's day when the ice echoed to the clicking hoofbeats of a swift-moving reindeer herd, and the breath of men and beasts smoked in the frosty air.

I awoke in the morning to a curious sound coming from the lake: a chorus of whistles and grunts that sounded like the last gasps of an ancient boiler. At first I was unable to identify the source of the noise. Then about a quarter of a mile away I saw the distinctive upright necks of whooper swans. In the same moment they saw me, and like a pair of vintage flying boats, they taxied laboriously across the water until their powerful wings gave their 20-pound bodies flying speed. Then, trumpeting in time with their wing-beats, they banked round in a wide circle and, still calling noisily, disappearing behind an island.

It was an encouraging start to the day, because not only are whooper swans increasingly rare in Lapland (some are shot for food, for sport and for collectors, others crash into power cables on their migratory flights), but their alertness rarely allows one to approach closer than a mile. The pair I had seen probably had a nest in the area, and by now would be tending their brood of gawky, dingy-looking young. In October, before the cygnets had moulted and assumed their gleaming white adult plumage, the parents would be demonstrating their eagerness to start the autumn migration. With wings unfurled and necks pumping like pistons, they would be standing on lake margins calling to each other and to other swans newly arrived from farther north. By the time the birch leaves had fallen and the first blizzards swept the lake, the air would be filled with the haunting bugle call of flocks of whooper swans as, invisible against the night sky, they flew south.

I could hardly avoid being aware of a host of other waterfowl. Flotillas of tufted duck, dapper in black and white, bobbed on the sunlit water. They are diving ducks, and at any one time half the flock was under water, to emerge like corks and wait their turn while the rest of the flock disappeared beneath the surface. Goldeneye, recognizable by their triangular heads, haunted the wooded fringes of the lake where they had finished nesting in holes high up in trees. Some way out from the shore, a male pintail dabbled for food, looking faintly ridiculous as it up-ended itself, head underwater and long tail sticking up.

Near the island where I had seen the swans disappear, I identified the low, cigar-shaped profile of a diver, a kind of avian submarine that can stay underwater for up to 15 minutes and descend to depths below one hundred feet. The diver was too distant for me to recognize which of the two breeding species commonly found in Lapland this specimen represented. But I recalled the spine-chilling cry I had heard the evening before and I concluded that it was a black-throated diver.

There were other ducks, too: mallard, scaup, teal, and a lone smew, here near the western limits of its breeding range. Like the swans they would all soon desert Lapland for the coasts, lakes and rivers of temperate Europe, and I wondered how many city-dwellers strolling through urban parks during the winter would realize that some of the ducks so tamely begging for scraps by ornamental lakes had spent the summer in this remote arctic setting.

Moving on a few miles, I passed Skogfoss, where members of the largest colony of house martins in Lapland were chasing mosquitoes over the river. Unfortunately, the martins left enough of these pests to trouble me maddeningly. One of the few hillocks in the Pasvik valley promised some relief from the mosquitoes, so I climbed it. The view westwards over the birch scrub was extensive, but what drew my eye even more compellingly was a pall of smoke across the Soviet Union's border. First I thought I was witnessing a forest fire, but then I saw that the smoke rose in regular columns and I realized it came from the chimneys of Nikel, an industrial town built in the midst of the taiga.

It may seem astonishing that a government should wish to build a large town in such inhospitable surroundings. But the region is rich in iron and nickel. In order to exploit these minerals the Russians are opening up the taiga, carving out new roads, draining bogs and building new towns. Big though it has become, Nikel is still a mere pin-prick in this vast wilderness and one could be forgiven for assuming that industrial development on Soviet territory is unlikely to have much effect on the Lapland environment. There is a latent threat, however. The thousands of square miles of taiga adjoining Lapland's border are a reservoir of wildlife, not only for Lapland but for all northern Europe. Destroy them, and the large annual influx of animals from the east, particularly of waders and waterfowl, would dwindle to a mere trickle.

Perhaps a more imminent threat to the balance of nature in the Pasvik valley is posed by the reindeer. The Lapps living in the valley are denied free movement across the strictly-guarded border that runs its length and so are forced to graze their herds in a restricted area throughout the year. Such a restriction is contrary, not only to Lapp custom but also to the migratory habits of their semi-domesticated reindeer, which are normally moved from one pasture to another in order not to strip the grazing grounds bare of the slow-growing lichens, their staple diet.

In the Pasvik valley the problem is compounded by the presence of a comparatively large and growing population of elk which, like reindeer, require an extensive feeding range. Elk do not compete with reindeer for grazing; they are taiga animals, browsers of twigs, leaves and aquatic plants. But they have prodigious appetites and usually move out of woodland before they have over-browsed it. In the Pasvik valley, however, their movements are restricted by the national border to the east and the barren plateau in the west, so they must crop the same habitat all year round. In a hard winter, therefore, the elk are forced to strip the bark from mature trees which, exposed to fungal attack will die, and also to eat young tree shoots, thus preventing the natural regeneration of the taiga vegetation.

These large, permanent populations of reindeer and elk, with their vulnerable calves, have attracted predators that once were rare or unknown in the Pasvik valley. Lynx, which had not been seen there before 1960, now lurk around the fringes of the reindeer herds; wolverines are increasing and spreading north; in severe winters, marauding wolves raid across the border from the Soviet Union. Because they help to cull the surplus elk and reindeer, these predators might seem welcome newcomers. They are certainly interesting additions to the valley fauna. The danger lies in the fact that the present abundance of food is unnatural. Should a population crash occur among the elk and reindeer, an over-population of predators would be forced to seek alternative food sources, which it is unlikely the valley could provide.

It was with this rather gloomy thought in mind that I completed my journey down the Pasvik valley. As the dull-red wooden buildings of Kirkenes came in sight, I recalled those columns of smoke rising out of the Russian taiga, and I could not help wondering what fate awaited the valley, and whether, in future years, the waters of the Pasvik would continue to run their unpolluted course from Inari down to the sea.

Invaders from the South

As spring dawns in Lapland, the frozen wastes are transformed into huge lakes or marshes, while offshore ice melts or floats away. Plants sprout, insects stir, and the birds that have spent the cold months outside the Arctic Circle come back into a burgeoning realm to join the snowy owl (*right*), one of the few of their kind that have been able to withstand the rigours of the northern winter.

The spring migrants turn Lapland into a vast breeding ground, and so relatively undisturbed is this northernmost outpost of the European wilderness that they can do so with little fear of man's interference.

Some birds spend the winter just outside the Arctic Circle, leaving them short distances to retrace when the weather improves. Whooper swans, for example, come largely from Scandinavia. They fly to the newly unfrozen lakes where waterweed is soon to be found growing in abundance. This provides the swans with their favourite food, and also ample material for building their bulky lakeside nests.

King and common eiders remain offshore, feeding on crabs, mussels and other saltwater creatures. Strangely, only the common eider comes ashore to breed, building a downy nest among the lush Lapland vegetation. Cormorants stay closer to the rocky shoreline, diving for fish and nesting in colonies on the cliffs or among the boulders.

Perhaps the most remarkable of the summer visitors are the waders, birds that may fly thousands of miles from their winter quarters. Among them are the whimbrels, which arrive in their flocks from as far away as Africa. They need time to recover from their tiring journey, and before moving inland to breed, spend long hours probing the soft coastal mud for the small animals on which they feed to regain strength.

A less gregarious species of wader, the red-necked phalarope, returns to Lapland from the open Atlantic Ocean in May; immediately it switches from its winter diet of plankton to one of insects and their larvae. And only a few weeks later, as the short Lapland summer fades into autumn, the red-necked phalarope, having raised its young in the north, is among the first to fly south again. This first departure takes place even before the end of July. One by one, other species follow suit, until the bitter winter cold turns Lapland once more into the lonely domain of the snowy owl.

An adult snowy owl, one of the few year-long avian inhabitants of Lapland, watches for the slightest movement that will betray a bird or mammal. When it sights its prey, the owl will take off on large rounded wings, gliding slowly before the final dash to secure its meal.

A whooper swan glides along the mirror-smooth surface of an arctic lake in spring. Such vegetation-bordered lakes provide its favourite nesting sites. The swan builds a large nest out of waterweed and grass and lays up to five eggs. The young are able to swim soon after hatching, but cannot fly until they are about two months old.

After its long flight from Africa, a whimbrel defends its Lapland nesting ground against other males that are also seeking territory. Breeding must be hurried so that the whimbrel can return south before the early frosts diminish its precious food supplies.

A red-necked phalarope searches the vegetation for insects. Although classified as waders, these birds spend most of the year on the open sea, coming ashore only during the summer breeding season. But they are very light and are occasionally swept inland by gales.

Flocks of king and common eiders (above) congregate on the open sea to feed on marine life. Such large gatherings are rare, however, and occur only in early spring in the Arctic Circle when enough ice has thawed to allow the birds to settle on the water before they disperse to their chosen breeding grounds.

A male king eider (right) in breeding plumage blends with the light reflections and the colour of the sea. His brilliant colouring is sharply contrasted with that of the mottled brown female, although in August he moults into an "eclipse" plumage in which he is flightless and a similar shade of brown.

Silhouetted against the arctic midnight sun, common cormorants roost on coastal rocks. In their search for food they swim in shallow waters close to the shore, keeping a lookout for shoals of fish. When prey are sighted, the birds dive in pursuit below the surface, remaining submerged for up to a minute. Emerging with a fish, they throw it into the air and then catch it head first before swallowing it.

6/ An Offshore Realm

*The islands lay on the glassy water, every rock
faithfully reflected so that it was almost impossible
to know which was the reality and which the reflection.*

HUGH BRANDON-COX/ *SUMMER OF A MILLION WINGS*

The fishing boat emerged from Saltfjord on Norway's northwest coast and when it met the broken swell of the open sea the flock of mewing gulls that had trailed in its wake all the way from harbour fell behind, leaving a single arctic tern as outrider. Gradually the port of Bodø became a blur on the receding coast until it was hidden from view behind the scattered skerries that fringe the mouth of the fjord. Soon, all that I could see of mainland Lapland were the ramparts of mountains beyond the port. Ahead the sea empty and it was not until we had sailed westwards for another hour that I saw a faint smudge on the horizon. The smudge grew, assumed shape and slowly resolved itself into a line of crests separated by the sea. These were the remote outliers of Lapland: the Lofoten Islands.

The boat was still too far away for me to identify individual islands, but the one dead ahead was almost certainly Vaerøy, my immediate destination, which meant that the long humps of rock south of it were part of the Røst group of islands, the southernmost of the inhabited Lofotens. Fading into the haze to the north was a scattered line of smaller stacks and outcrops, links in a much larger chain that runs north for more than one hundred miles to form an archipelago along the coast of western Lapland. Subterranean remnants of the Lofoten system even penetrate the arctic as far as Spitzbergen, the Norwegian archipelago about 400 miles to the north.

The Norwegians call this archipelago the Lofoten Wall. But the gaps that separate each link in the island chain, and the crenellated peaks that emerge, sometimes sheer from the sea, give it more the appearance of a line of battlements. Vaerøy, which we were fast approaching, is not the highest of the islands, yet my first sight of it was impressive enough. As the boat drew nearer its looming bulk, I saw an implacable mass of grey rock, its base fretted with foaming inlets and gaunt headlands. A bay swept southwards to the tiny village of Mostad, nestling under cliffs that rose to a thousand feet and so precipitous that they seemed about to topple over and engulf the houses below. Not a single tree was visible, and most of the island vegetation appeared to be a matted skin of rank grasses and heather. Yet there was evidence of a greater fertility: some of the sheltered slopes were covered in luxuriant turf greener than any I had seen elsewhere in Lapland.

Geologically, the Lofoten Islands are a branch of the Scandinavian mountain chain, and they are composed of the same granites and gneisses I had seen on the Lyngen peninsula. They form the region's first line of defence against the Atlantic: and they are among the most northerly places in the world to derive benefit from the Gulf Stream. This current of relatively warm water, which has its source in the Caribbean, flows northeast across the Atlantic, accompanied by warm, moisture-laden winds. South of Newfoundland the Stream splits into two and while the western half goes north to Greenland, the eastern half, now called the North Atlantic Drift, wanders towards northern Europe before petering out in the Arctic Ocean.

The Gulf Stream's effects on the Lofotens are dramatic. Although the archipelago is situated north of the Arctic Circle, its climate displays none of the seasonal extremes that characterize interior Lapland. Winters are relatively mild, summers cool, and the sky is almost permanently overcast with sombre, grey clouds. Precipitation is heavy, about 40 inches annually, but comparatively little falls as snow, and the small proportion that does is soon melted away by westerly winds sweeping in from the Atlantic.

The same current that tempers the rigours of the arctic climate also supplies the Lofotens with their main harvest—fish. The sea around the islands is like a broth composed of countless billions of minute animal and vegetable organisms—the plankton. It has been estimated that an acre of the North Atlantic yields a crop of about one ton of plankton annually, and reaping that crop is one of the densest fish populations in the world. In turn, the huge schools of cod that feed and spawn in these waters support a major fishing industry in the islands. The trawler-men, however, must compete with other fishers of the ocean: the whales, seals and sea-birds.

It was sea-birds rather than fish that had lured me to the Lofotens. Almost every island, stack and skerry is an avian metropolis, each cliff a high-rise tenement teeming with birds. In the days ahead I planned to explore the colonies of Vaerøy and the neighbouring islands of Røst. Then before going home I intended to leave the islands, return to the mainland and visit the bird colony at Ekkerøy, a tiny peninsula in Varangerfjord, on the northeastern coast of Lapland.

As the fishing boat entered the bay that marks the eastern flank of Vaerøy it disturbed a massed fleet of guillemots riding on the water as if in some naval review. They took off with a rapid running movement of their webbed feet, then, wings whirring, they circled to return to one of the bird colonies along the bay.

One of the things I hoped to see on Vaerøy was a sea eagle's nest. Until the beginning of the 20th Century, this majestic bird, with its massive hooked beak, eight-foot wingspan and white tail, was a relatively common sight along the coast of Europe. But sheep farmers blamed it for killing lambs and drove it from its southern haunts. In Britain it was extinct by 1910. Even in the comparatively remote Lofotens a price was put on its head. Since a trapper could catch up to a hundred birds during autumn and winter, the breeding population soon plummeted. Not until the 1960s did the sea eagle receive legal protection in Norway. But by then the surviving population had to contend with a new and deadlier threat—that posed by marine pollution.

The morning after I landed, an islander took me by boat to one of the sea eagle's strongholds and, standing on a shingle beach at the foot of a towering cliff, pointed out an eyrie beneath a bulging overhang 600 feet up. The adult sea eagles had raised one young bird, the islander told me, but the fully-fledged eaglet had already left the nest. Farther along the coast we clambered up a steep headland: at the top, set among a jumble of rocks, was a pit that had once been used to trap sea eagles. It was simply a narrow hollow about ten feet long, with an observation slit at one end and a detachable roof fashioned from a stone slab. With my guide's help I pulled back the cover and climbed inside.

The interior was damp, cold and cramped. Through the slit I could see the flat rock a few yards away on which the bait, usually a piece of bloody meat, was placed and tied by a rope that led into the pit. An eagle circling high above the island would be sure to spot it and

The fisherman told me that puffins were still captured and eaten by the islanders, although on nothing like the scale of bygone years. I must have looked slightly dubious at the thought of anyone choosing to eat what I assumed must be rather fishy fare, but he assured me that young puffins, braised in a thick gravy and served with boiled potatoes and jam sauce, made a delicious change from the cod that is the staple diet of the islanders. At one time, he told me, tens of thousands of puffins were killed annually and their carcasses preserved in salt for winter eating. Amazingly, such slaughter did not endanger the puffins survival as a species here; there are still something like three million on the islands of Røst alone.

That night the weather displayed the unpredictability for which the Lofotens are famous. Rain beat at the windows of the cottage where I was staying, a howling wind threatened to lift off the corrugated iron roof, and its roar mingled with the crash of waves breaking on the coast. If the bad weather persisted I could be stranded on Vaeröy for days, unable to make the two-hour boat journey to the islands of Röst. When I awoke, I found to my relief that the storm had blown itself out. Scudding clouds still hid the island peaks, and my first sight of a choppy, lead-coloured sea induced a momentary queasiness, but the skipper of the boat I had hired assured me that for the Lofotens, conditions were unusually calm.

I had faith in his assurances. The seafaring Lofoten islanders, trained to recognize the many moods of the sea from early childhood, must be among the best seamen in the world. They need to be: the waters around the islands, forced through narrow channels by the rising and falling tides, are a maze of treacherous rip-currents. Just north of Vaerøy is the most famous of them all, the Moskenstrom, better known as the Maelstrom. In his "A Descent into the Maelstrom", Edgar Allan Poe describes this phenomenon as a "terrific funnel, whose interior . . . was a smooth, shining and jet-black wall of water, inclined to the horizon at an angle of some 45°, speeding dizzily round and round with a swaying and sweltering motion". Whirlpools are a recognized hazard around the islands, and as we sailed away from Vaerøy in a fragile-looking fishing boat, I uneasily recalled some lines from a Victorian sailing guide that stated bluntly, "boats and men have been drawn by these vortices and much loss of life has resulted".

But apart from an occasional protest from my stomach, the journey was uneventful, and by midday the boat was threading its way between the small, scattered islands of the Røst group. Skirting Røst, the largest of them, we passed between reefs on which were drawn up lines of cormorants, their outspread wings giving them the appearance of dirty, tattered washing. They were drying their wings between fishing expeditions. Unlike that of other sea-birds, the cormorant's plumage is not completely waterproof and it becomes waterlogged after long immersion.

Rounding the southern tip of the island I saw Vedøya, our destination, and soon afterwards my nostrils were hit by the awful stench of guano and my ears bombarded with a concert of cries from the bird colonies. Kittiwakes drifted like snowflakes around the cliffs; puffins and guillemots launched themselves off ledges like short-winged projectiles; while above them, menacing in black and white, black-backed gulls wheeled watchfully, hoping to benefit from our intrusion by snapping up any fledgling left untended by its parents.

We landed in a sheltered cove and made our way up a steep slope whitewashed with bird droppings. Where soil had accumulated between the rocks the guano had acted as a fertilizer, and rich grass and colourful blue-petalled Jacob's ladder and yellow arctic poppies abounded. High above this luxuriance we stopped to look down. The birds ignored us now and had resumed the ceaseless fluttering activity that gives a sea-bird colony the air of a busy railway station. Far below us, a raft of guillemots floated on the water; and as we watched, its numbers were swelled by other individuals flying down from the rock ledges. They seemed to be assembling at some pre-arranged meeting place, for once the last bird had joined them the whole flock took off in unison, heading out to their feeding grounds, while a few lone puffins came whirring back to the island.

My attention was diverted by some smoky-grey birds cutting effortless circles in the air. Without moving their wings they rode the updraught spilling over the cliff top, and when they lost momentum, they glided steeply down to the sea to meet the air currents forced upwards by the movements of the waves. These birds were fulmars: like their close relatives, the albatrosses, they are truly oceanic birds, perfect flying machines that can stay aloft for days, even weeks, at a stretch, following the fishing boats and whalers to scavenge on the rich pickings of offal thrown overboard.

The fulmar has one unattractive habit. When threatened at its nest it opens its beak wide, displaying a purple mouth, and hiccups out a stream of yellowish stomach oil with an indescribably foul smell. Six feet is reported to be the extreme range of this defence weapon, but on

Hundreds of seabirds crowd jagged cliffs overlooking Varangerfjord in Norwegian Lapland. The cormorants can be distinguished by their black plumage from the smaller grey-and-white kittiwakes that make up the majority of this summer colony. Unlike most gulls, which use depressions in the ground for their nests, kittiwakes build solid nests of mud, grass or seaweed, to prevent their eggs from falling off the ledges.

the occasions when I have climbed down to fulmars' nests I have always allowed another yard or so for safety. Fulmar chicks possess this doubtful attribute from a very early age, and before they learn when and when not to use it, they even squirt the fluid at their parents. The adults bear this indignity with remarkable equanimity. In fact, the fluid is not so disgusting to the fulmar. It appears to play an important part in their courtship rituals, being passed from beak to beak as if it were some precious gift. Still, trespassing birds would do better to avoid it: when it covers a bird's feathers it strips away the water-proofing as effectively as crude oil. Sea-birds thus afflicted are doomed to die a lingering death by drowning after alighting on the water.

Petrels, swallow-sized relatives of the fulmar, are another group of Lofoten bird species that discharge this stomach oil. Like the fulmar, they are classified as tube-noses; they possess tubular extensions on their nostrils. Some oil is ejected through the tubes, but their main purpose is to act as vents for the salt that accumulates in the bodies of these ocean wanderers.

The islands of Røst offer breeding sites to two species of petrel: Leach's petrel and the storm petrel. The forked tail, greater size and buoyant flight of Leach's petrel make it the more conspicuous of the two; but the storm petrel, although Europe's smallest sea-bird, has a reputation out of all proportion to its size and rather dowdy appearance. To sailors it is known by an alternative name, Mother Carey's chicken—"Mother Carey" being a corruption of *Mater Cara*, the Virgin Mary. The 18th and 19th Century mariners regarded storm petrels as harbingers of doom because of their almost magical appearance at the onset of storms. The birds were, of course, riding the winds ahead of the storm.

Even these far-wandering birds have to find land for breeding, and I had been told that storm petrels were raising young on the islands of Trenyken and Hernyken. These were their most northerly breeding grounds, only a few miles south of Vedøya. I persuaded the owner of the fishing boat to take me there and late in the evening we set sail from Vedøya heading south. It was not long before I saw my first petrel. After witnessing the aerial mastery of the fulmar I felt that the storm petrel cut a rather sorry figure. It almost seemed injured as it fluttered feebly between the waves, occasionally lowering its webbed feet to splash along the surface, as if trying to relieve the strain on its wings by walking. Each time it dived I gave it up for lost, yet it always re-emerged; and I realized that its weak fluttering flight was normal, and that the action of its feet stirred up the plankton on which it was feeding.

Built up by sediment deposited in layers on the sea bed millennia ago, these sandstone cliffs on the coast of Porsangerfjord, in northern Lapland, expose the sedimentary strata that have long since solidified into bands of hard and soft stone. Their worn and serrated profile has been caused by the incessant battering of the Arctic Ocean.

Even so, I could not understand how so small a bird could survive a storm at sea, let alone spend the entire winter far out in the Atlantic Ocean, as the petrel does. But the worse the weather, the less effort petrels seem to expend, riding as they do the air currents in the troughs of the waves. Other mysteries still surround this bird. Nobody knows how they rest at sea or whether they sleep; and their breeding behaviour is unlike that of other birds, as I discovered when we reached their colony, a few hours after setting off.

When we landed on Trenyken dusk had fallen. With only an electric torch to light our path, we stumbled and groped our way to the colony, treading warily in case we stumbled on the breeding burrows in the darkness. But we soon discovered there was no need for such caution, for we heard the birds long before we saw them. From all sides rose an uncanny twittering and croaking, quite unlike any bird cries I had heard before. In the dim light I could not make out the source of the sounds: they seemed to issue from all around us, confusing my sense of direction and creating a Hitchcock-like atmosphere of suspense. Then, as my eyes adjusted to the gloom, I made out dim shapes flitting through the air, crying like lost souls to their mates waiting crouched at the entrances to their burrows.

The birds were returning from their feeding grounds with food for the fledglings. Such nocturnal activity enables the petrels, whose weak legs make them almost helpless on the ground, to escape the attention of predators, such as gulls: it may also arise from the greater concentration of surface plankton at night. Possibly they use their cries as directional signals to guide them back to their nests, but recent research has proved that petrels are among the very few birds to possess a sense of smell; perhaps this, too, plays an important part in their ability to home in on breeding burrows. Although the storm petrels nest late in the year, like the puffins they have an unusually long fledgling period—nearly nine weeks. The young, hatched in late summer, are sometimes not on the wing until December. Yet while the animals on the mainland are scratching a meagre living in the arctic winter darkness, the young petrels grow so fat that they are unable to fly even when almost fully grown. At this stage of their development, the parents stop feeding them and, left to fast for several days, the young finally scrabble out of their burrows and, notwithstanding the fact that their burrow existence has left them with weak wings, launch themselves as an unruly and unpractised squadron round the coast of Lapland.

This breeding cycle, so out of key with those of birds on the mainland, reflects the seasonal rhythm of plankton growth in the surrounding waters. In May, the sun is strong enough to allow the phytoplankton (vegetable plankton) to photosynthesize, grow and reproduce. As spring gives way to early summer, an explosion of plankton production occurs, providing rich feeding for the fish and sea-birds, most of which breed at this time. Within a month or two, however, the rate of plankton production slows down. But here, where the cold currents of the high arctic seas meet the warmer currents of the North Atlantic Drift, an upsurge of water dredges a new supply of nutrients off the sea bed to stimulate further plankton growth. Along these polar fronts, plankton occurs in large quantities into the autumn and yields a late harvest to nourish the young storm petrels.

Reaping the harvest with the petrels is a massive fish population; and to the inhabitants of coastal Lapland, the word "fish" invariably means the Atlantic cod. If the Lofoten islanders designed a national flag, it would bear the symbol of a cod, for the economy of this sea-girt region is based on this most valuable food fish, just as that of the Mountain Lapps is founded on the reindeer. Near every cottage on the islands I saw racks on which salted cod were hung up to dry; and while sailing south to the petrels' colony, we had passed dozens of fishermen line-fishing for the species. My guide agreed to take me with him on his next fishing trip.

We left Vaerøy next morning, heading east to the fishing grounds. As we entered the open sea, the skipper explained that at this time of year most of the big adult cod, which can reach a length of six feet, would be feeding in deep water to the north; only a few individuals would be left in these parts. They arrive at their spawning grounds off the Lofotens in January or February, he said, lay their eggs, then gradually disperse northwards round the coasts of Finnmark and Spitzbergen. He explained: each female lays up to five million eggs that float for about 20 days before they hatch (of these, perhaps, only two will develop into mature fish). The tiny larval fish then become a part of the animal plankton, drifting aimlessly near the surface of the sea and being preyed upon by other fish and sea-birds. After two-and-a-half months the cod fry sink to the sea bed where they grow rapidly. By now, said the skipper, the cod hatched this year would be about five inches long.

We had sailed only a short distance before my guide pointed to a large blue jellyfish floating near the boat. There, under its trailing tentacles, were a group of this season's cod. At first I assumed they were seeking protection beneath the broad bell of the jellyfish. But the skipper told me they were attracted by particles of food dropped by their host as it transferred prey from its stinging tentacles to its mouth. Like dogs snapping up morsels beneath their master's table, the young cod were taking advantage of the jellyfish's messy eating habits.

With the first gales of winter the growing cod would migrate north to the Barents Sea and seek more substantial fare. Any bottom-dwelling fish or invertebrate small enough and sluggish enough for them to catch would be eagerly devoured. After two years the young cod would undertake the first of their winter migrations, not to the Lofotens, but following the massive shoals of capelin—a herring-like fish related to the salmon—to their spawning grounds in Lapland's coastal waters off Finnmark. For several months the cod would plunder the capelin shoals until their prey moved into deeper water and hunger forced them back to the Barents Sea. For five or six years the cod would make these seasonal migrations until, at the age of seven years and approaching five feet in length, they would be mature enough to return to the Lofotens to spawn and give rise to the next generation.

When we reached the fishing grounds, the skipper threw out his weighted lines armed with baited hooks, and while we waited for the deep-feeding fish to bite, he told me of some of the other creatures that haunt the depths around the Lofotens. There was the pogge, he said, a strange-sounding fish whose armoured, broad-headed, whip-tailed body reminded him of a prehistoric lizard. He described another fish he had caught near weed-beds—the evil looking catfish whose powerful jaws rimmed with rows of teeth can crush the shells of bottom-living molluscs. Their taste belied their appearance, he assured me, although he admitted that before selling them he cut off their ugly heads. He spoke also of the gurnard, a fish that had surprised him when he landed one because it had made a low grunting noise as it floundered in the bottom of his boat.

Often, he said, the waters around the Lofotens were invaded by species from foreign waters. He described how, on calm summer evenings, he had seen the water near his boat erupt as needle-shaped garfish jumped high above the surface to escape pursuing tunny or dolphins. Once he had seen an oarfish swimming like a 20-foot-long silver ribbon on edge, its dorsal fin a blazing red line down the length of the body, and on another occasion he had watched the opah, an iridescent fish with a round, moon-like face, greedily sucking up a squid.

Sometimes more menacing creatures appeared around his boat. One blustery day in spring, he had seen a towering black fin break the water, and as he watched, it was joined by another and another until four sail-like dorsal fins cleaved the water in circles round his flimsy craft. They were killer whales, attracted by the same shoal of cod that he was fishing, but after a few anxious minutes they made off towards a near-by island that harboured a colony of grey seals, a favourite prey. Another time he had experienced an equally unnerving few moments when a 10-foot-long Greenland shark, the only arctic member of the family, used the keel of his boat as a rubbing post.

The skipper finished talking and we sat in silence. Rhythmically he pulled at the line to attract the fish's attention; by noon we had caught four fine cod, bearded monsters with a thick insulating layer of slime on their bodies. We started back and on the way the skipper pointed out shoals of transparent young eels, or elvers, newly arrived after their 3,000-mile, three-year journey from their birthplace in the Sargasso Sea. Entering the bay, the skipper scooped up something from the water and showed me what looked like a tiny pale glove, bloated as though it still contained a hand. It was called "dead man's fingers", he said, and surprised me by telling me that it was a species of soft coral. We reached harbour tired and hungry after our long fishing trip, and that night we dined regally on the cod we had caught.

Next day I left Vaerøy on the last stage of my Lapland journey, travelling north, via Tromsø and the Lyngen peninsula to Ekkerøy, in Varangerfjord. Driving through the mountain passes that I had explored three months before, I saw with a shock of realization that the snow line on the peaks was lower than on my last visit. As I travelled on, the sun lost its warmth and I awoke each morning to find the ground beaded with frost. The Lapland summer, so brief and so intense, was drawing very rapidly to a close.

Farther on, I stopped briefly at North Cape, popularly supposed to be the most northerly point in Europe and the goal of many tourists, expecting something tawdry and cheapened by commercialism. Yet, standing on the 1,000-foot-high, biscuit-hued cliffs among luxury coaches and sightseers, I was strangely impressed. The sea rolling away to the north, 600 miles towards the Polar ice, remained a wilderness, daunting and defeating.

I reached Ekkerøy late one afternoon and immediately contacted a local ornithologist who knew the area well. At first he treated me with suspicion, and I discovered why—egg-collectors had ravaged nests in

Varanger that summer, taking eggs of rough-legged buzzards, merlins, red-necked phalarope and the rare smew. Fortunately I had a letter of introduction from my good friend Edvard Barth of Oslo, an authority on Lapland's birds; and once convinced of my *bona fides*, the ornithologist promised to show me what he obviously regarded as one of the wonders of the bird world.

My first reaction to Ekkerøy was one of disappointment. Compared with the awesome cliffs of Vaerøy, its slopes, although steep, were small and unimposing, and, at first sight, did not appear to support the teeming bird life I had seen in the Lofotens. When I voiced my doubts to my guide, he merely smiled, as if to say: "Wait and see".

We began our expedition at sea-level where red-throated pipits and a white wagtail hovered above the high grass to snatch insects out of the air. Then we worked our way up a grassy slope that levelled out on a promontory. To the north I saw a sandy shore, deserted except for a pair of hooded crows beachcombing for shellfish. To the south was a headland about a hundred feet high, the home, my companion said, of 50,000 kittiwakes. As we walked towards this point, my first clue to the presence of a bird colony was the profusion of orange lichen that is reputed to grow only where gull droppings have fallen. When once again I was assailed by the stench of guano, I forgot the smell as I beheld thousands of kittiwakes lining the ledges below.

Craning over the edge of the cliff, I was almost deafened by the strident, syncopated chorus of Kitti-WAAK; Kitti-WAAK. I could make out every detail of the birds' plumage: the white head and tail, the delicate pearly-grey colour of their backs, and the inky-black wing tips. At such close quarters I could see the purplish rims that surrounded the eyes of the young and the dark bands on the backs of their necks.

I had often seen kittiwakes foraging for nesting materials at the beginning of the breeding season and after watching them winging straight to their nesting ledges, had admired the sort of homes they make. So it was no surprise to find that the nest I now climbed down to examine seemed to be cemented to the ledge by dried mud and had obviously been built with care. Seaweed, grasses and lichens were the main components, all compacted by much treading of webbed feet. It was a more aesthetically pleasing structure than the nests of greater black-backed gulls, which decorate their breeding places with grisly remains of their victims. But it still had one drawback: it was tenanted by voracious fleas and flies that crept over me.

Because Ekkerøy is not one of the towering stacks that also accommodate predatory black-backed gulls, sea-eagles and ravens, the kittiwakes co-existed in comparative harmony. Members of the colony returning from fishing expeditions were allowed to eat their catch without being molested by their tightly-packed neighbours. The colony was the noisiest I had ever come across. Still, it was a sociable clamour, reminiscent of a classroom when the teacher is absent.

At the foot of the cliff the ledges were stacked with what looked like rows of old umbrellas, reminding me of a lost property office. Through binoculars I identified the "umbrellas" as a colony of black guillemots, standing so close together that their large white wing patches were obscured. Unlike the kittiwakes, they stood in motionless glum silence, staring lugubriously out to sea like a convention of undertakers waiting for a shipwreck. Presently a gap appeared in one of their ranks as a bird flipped itself into the sea, and with a shock of excitement I recognized a bird with a shorter, stouter beak than its neighbours and with a thin, pale line along its upper mandible. It was a Brünnich's guillemot, a species found nowhere else in Europe except Iceland—and seeing it, I felt the elation of confronting, unexpectedly, a new and rare bird.

Convinced now that Ekkerøy was well worth exploring, I needed no prompting when my companion suggested we make our way down to the western shore to look for marine ducks. Emerging on to the beach, we surprised turnstones levering pebbles over in their search for food. When they saw us, they took a few rapid steps, their legs scuttling round and round, and launched themselves into the air with twittering cries. Farther along, I saw the pied plumage and blood-red bills of a group of oyster-catchers, animatedly upbraiding a purple sandpiper that had strayed on to their feeding territory.

The first duck we spotted was a male goosander, whose long, narrow toothed bill and cigar-shaped body called to mind what birds are from an evolutionary viewpoint: warmed up reptiles with feathers. Scanning the sea I picked out a pair of long-tailed ducks, diving birds that can submerge to depths of a hundred feet; farther out was a pair of eider ducks followed by three immature birds swimming line astern. I knew that four species of eider occur at Ekkerøy during the year: the common, king, spectacled and Steller's, but I could not tell which these were at such a distance. The ducks cruised closer, occasionally disappearing beneath the waves as they dived for molluscs or seaweed, and I now realized from the drake's pure white back and black-capped head that the birds were common eiders. The drake's plumage, so conspicuous

Suspended in mid-air with almost symmetrical precision, an adult arctic tern hovers over the sea on the lookout for fish. The long, pointed wings beat powerfully to hold the bird aloft while the spread tail acts as a balancing rudder. Once a fish has been sighted, the tern folds its wings, flips up its tail and plummets down in a headlong dive.

compared with the dowdy, uniform brown of the female, is a powerful mating symbol; it is also, unfortunately, a beacon for such predators as peregrines and gyr falcons which, hunting entirely by sight, are constantly on the look-out for a tell-tale flicker of black and white wings.

Male eiders are powerful birds, strong fliers and divers that for most of the year can evade predators. But during their period of eclipse, when they shed all their primary feathers at once and thus lose the power of flight, they are particularly vulnerable. For this reason, their plumage during this time is almost as drab as the females'. For added protection, they desert their breeding grounds and congregate in a safe place until new feathers have grown.

A few minutes after my encounter with the common eiders, a low crooning sound attracted me to a shallow lagoon where not just one but dozens of Steller's eider were feeding. When they saw us they took off with harsh quacks that changed into a whistling note as they circled overhead, displaying the warm russet of their breasts. The lagoon was left to a single arctic tern quartering the water for food. Like a ghostly white reflection it flickered over the surface, red bill pointing downwards, narrow boomerang-shaped wings winnowing as it hovered for a second, then side-slipped to another point. A slightly longer hover, a sudden darting dive, and the tern's beak just kissed the surface to emerge with a gleaming fish.

At that moment an arctic skua that had been soaring buoyantly near by uttered a chattering cry and swept down, hawk-like, on the smaller bird. Like a matador side-stepping a bull, the tern avoided the skua's first rush, and made a beeline for the open sea. But the piratical bird was persistent and, swinging round, dashed after the tern, matching every twist and turn the victim made in its efforts to escape. Backwards and forwards the birds flew, the skua effectively cutting off the tern's escape route and driving it lower and lower until its wings skimmed the sea. Finally, knowing it could not outdistance its pursuer, the tern opened its mouth and dropped the fish. The skua broke off the chase to catch the morsel as it fell down.

Soon the arctic terns of Ekkerøy would begin their annual moult, a gradual process that, unlike the moult of eiders, does not prevent them flying. In fact, it heralds their southwards migration, the greatest journey undertaken by any bird, from the arctic to the Antarctic. The total distance they cover each year is about 22,000 miles, and this they do at an average of 150 miles a day. They hold another record, too: they spend the summer in the perpetual daylight of the arctic and escape the dark winter of the north in the Antarctic—thus enjoying more hours of daylight over eight months than any other bird. The arctic terns are accompanied on their long southward flight by the arctic skuas which also winter in the Antarctic.

I spent my last day on Ekkerøy alone. In the north, shafts of sunlight broke through clouds shredded by a chill polar wind, and played on the spume whipped from the crests of the waves. The waves were too violent to allow ducks to swim, but on the wind-lashed beach, waders huddled disconsolately together, not feeding, heads turned and beaks buried in their ruffled plumage, waiting for that mysterious signal that would urge them south. Leaning into the wind, collar turned up against stinging showers of sleet, I battled my way up to the kittiwake colony for a final look—only to find the ledges deserted of almost all the adult birds. Left behind were the immature birds, wearing a woebegone, abandoned look.

From my vantage point on the clifftop, it was difficult to imagine that the sullen-looking fells across the fjord, now drained of all colour, had only a few weeks before been teeming with life. They looked cold and bare; almost overnight the Lapland summer had ended. As I walked back to pack, a lone arctic tern appeared, making little headway against the buffeting wind, gaining height slowly. Then, when it was so high that it appeared as a white star, it seemed to abandon its battle with the elements. For a split-second it held its position in the teeth of the gale, then a sudden gust caught it, spun it round like an autumn leaf and whipped it down wind. I saw the pale glimmer of its wings for a moment more, then it disappeared, lost in the sky to the south.

Facets of a Frozen World

Winter comes early to Lapland: by the end of September the long, light summer days have shortened and the mild air cools sharply. The darkness and cold gradually increase and by the middle of January temperatures plummet to —15° F. or below. Coupled with the cold are blizzards and snowfalls that draw a veil of snow and ice over the silent landscape.

But unlike the massive ice-sheets that blanketed the far north during the last Ice Age, the arrival of winter brings to Lapland a subtle transformation, enhancing rather than obliterating its beauty. It creates the delicate and minute crystals of hoar frost that edge trees, shrubs and dead leaves, fringes twigs and branches with icicles, freezes water into surrealist sculptures (right) and turns lakes and fjords into shimmering mirrors or opaque pavements of white and blue.

The cold lasts well into May. But with the onrush of spring, the days lengthen, temperatures rise and the ice begins to melt. The ice goes through permutation after permutation, as though some restless sculptor were continually refining and polishing his work. And then one day it is gone and the land, so long its prisoner, is at last set free.

BOULDER ICE FORMING IN A MOUNTAIN STREAM

CONVOLUTED ICE

ICICLE COMBS

ICE FRACTURED BY TIDE AND WIND INTO GEOMETRIC SHAPES

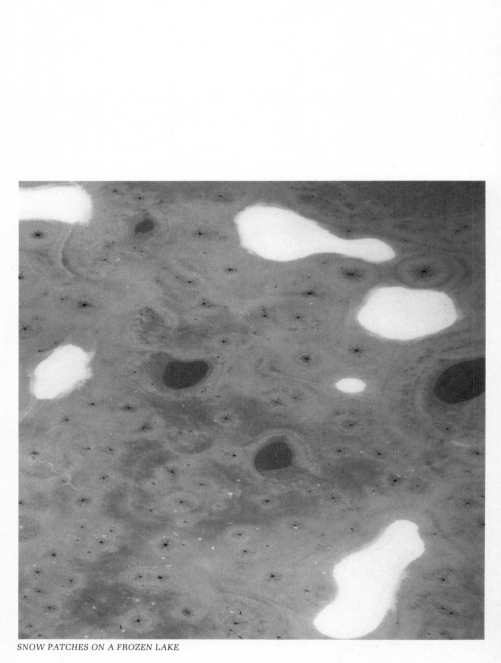

SNOW PATCHES ON A FROZEN LAKE

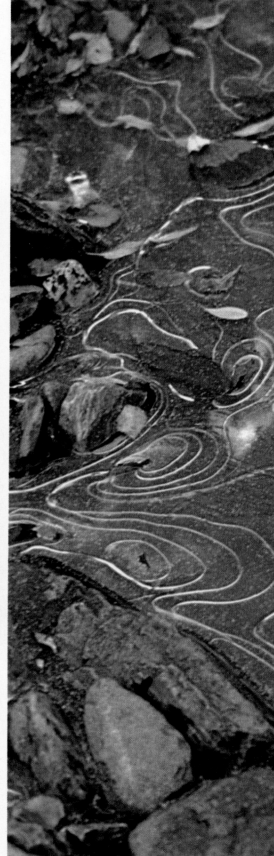

LEAVES TRAPPED IN RIPPLED ICE

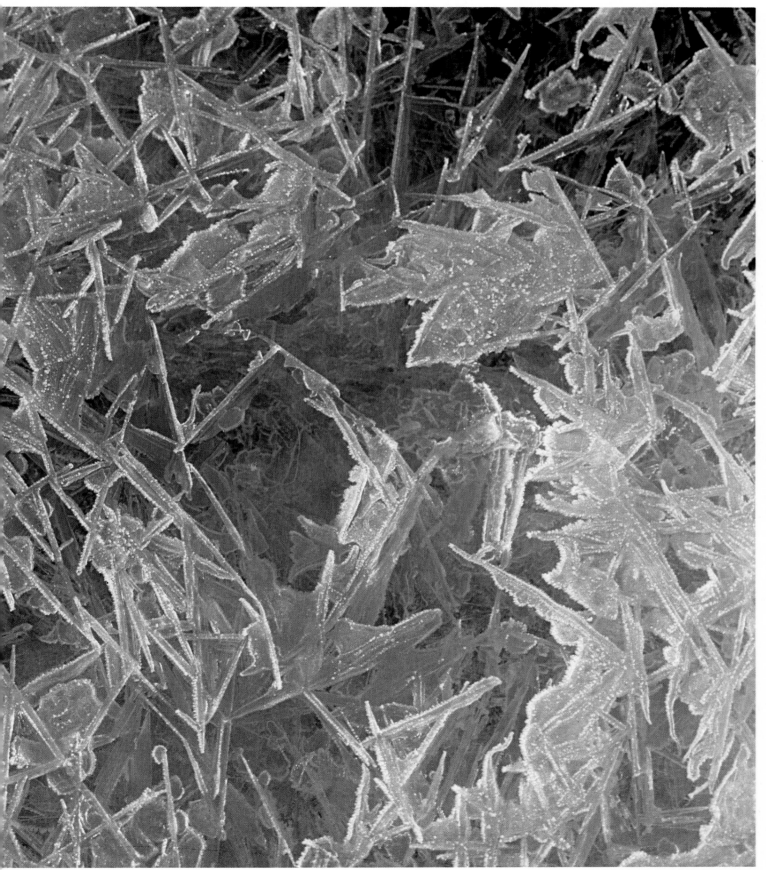

SPIKY CRYSTALS OF HOAR FROST

Bibliography

Bang, Preben, *Animal Tracks and Signs.* Collins, 1974.

Blunt, Wilfred, *The Compleat Naturalist, A Life of Linnaeus.* Collins, 1971.

Bosi, Roberto, *The Lapps.* Thames and Hudson, 1960.

Brandon-Cox, Hugh, *Summer of a Million Wings.* David Charles, 1974.

Brown, Alison Leadley, *Ecology of Fresh Water.* Heinemann, 1971.

Burton, Maurice, *Animals of Europe.* Eurobook, 1973.

Clegg, John, *Freshwater Life.* Frederic Warne, 1974.

Collinder, Björn, *The Lapps.* Princeton University Press, 1949.

Crottet, Robert, *Lapland.* Enrique Meridez, Hugh Evelyn Ltd., 1968.

Curry-Lindahl, Kai, *Sarek, Stora Sjöfallet Padjelanta.* Rydahls Boktryckert AB, 1968.

Curry-Lindahl, Kai, *Europe: A Natural History.* Random House, 1964.

Douglas, John, *Arctic Highway.* David and Charles, 1972.

Dröscher, Vitus B., *The Magic of the Senses.* W. H. Allen, 1969.

Duncan, Ursula K., *Introduction to British Lichens.* T. Buncle and Co., 1970.

Freuchen, Peter and Salomonsen, Finn *The Arctic Year.* Jonathan Cape, 1959 de la Fuente, Dr. Félix Rodriguez, *Rare Animals of the Wild Regions.* Orbis, 1974.

Gaskell, T. F., *The Gulf Stream.* Cassell, 1972.

Gilliard, E. Thomas, *Living Birds of the World.* Hamish Hamilton Ltd., 1965.

Gjaerevoll, Olav and Jørgensen, Reider, *Mountain Flowers of Scandinavia.* F. Bruns Bokhandels Forlag, 1972.

Graf, Jakob, *Animal Life of Europe.* Frederick Warne and Co., 1968.

Heinzel, H., Fitter, R., and Parslow, J., *The Birds of Britain and Europe.* William Collins and Son, 1974.

Herald, Earl S., *Living Fishes of the World.* Hamish Hamilton, 1972.

Holtehahl, Olaf, *Geology of Norway.* Norges Geologiske Undersökelse, 1960.

Hvarfner, Harald, *Hunting and Fishing.* "Nordic Symposium on Life in a Traditional Hunting and Fishing Milieu in Prehistoric Times and up to the Present Day." Norrbottens Museum, 1965.

Irving, Laurence, *Arctic Life of Birds and Mammals.* Springer-Verag, 1972.

Irwin, John L., *The Finns and The Lapps, How they Live and Work.* David and Charles, 1973.

Kilpi, Mikko, *Lapland in Colour.* Tammi, 1974.

Kurten, Björn, *The Ice Age.* G. P. Putnam's Sons, 1972.

Lister, R. P., *A Journey in Lapland—The Hard Way to Haparanda.* Chapman and Hall, 1965.

Lundquist, Gösta and Thaning, Olof, *Lapland.* Albert Bonniers Förlag, 1960.

Lynam, Edward, *The Carta Marina of Olaus Magnus, Venice 1539 & Rome 1572.* Tall Tree Library, 1949.

Magnus, Olaus, *A Compendious History of the Goths, Swedes and Vandals, and Other Northern Nations.* Humphrey Mosely, George Sawbridge, Henry Twiford, 1658.

Major, Alan P., *Coast, Estuary and Seashore Life.* John Gifford, 1973.

Manker, Ernst, *People of Eight Seasons.* C. A. Watts, 1965.

Marsden, Walter, *The Lemming Year.* Chatto and Windus, 1964.

Mellanby, Helen, *Animal Life in Fresh Water.* Methuen, 1963.

Muus, Bent, J., *Freshwater Fish of Britain and Europe.* Collins, 1971.

Nesheim, Asbjørn, *Introducing the Lapps.* Johan Grundt Tanum Forlag, 1971.

Nethersole-Thompson, Desmond, *The Greenshank.* Collins, 1971.

Nickels, Sylvie, *Finland Travellers Guide.* Jonathan Cape, 1965.

Nilsson, Edvin, *Sarek, Lapland's Wild-Life Sanctuary.* Bonniers, 1971.

Østren, G., Haakensen, N., and Melander, *Glacier Atlas of Northern Scandi— V navia.* Norges Vassdrags-og Elektrisitetsvesen og Stockholm Universitet, 1973.

Polunin, Oleg, *Flowers of Europe. A Field Guide.* Oxford University Press, 1969.

Poutvaara, Matti, *Lappi Lappland,* Werner Söderström Osakeyhtiö, 1957.

Pruitt, William O., *Animals of the North.* Harper and Row, 1967.

Richardson, David H. S., *The Vanishing Lichens.* David and Charles, 1975.

Ruong, Israel, *The Lapps in Sweden.* Swedish Institute for Cultural Relations, 1967.

Sanderson, Ivan T., *Living Mammals of the World.* Hamish Hamilton, 1969.

Schefferus, J., *The History of Lapland.* Oxford, 1674.

Smith, Bayliss S., *Wild Wings to the Northlands.* H. F. and G. Witherby Ltd., 1970.

Stonehouse, Bernard, *Animals of the Arctic. The Ecology of the Far North.* Ward Lock Ltd., 1971.

Sutherland, Halliday, *Lapland Journey.* Geoffrey Bles, 1938.

Taylor, R. J. F., *Sterna.* "Notes on the Birds of Finnmark." Feb., 1957.

Utsi, Mikel, Man. "The Reindeer-Breeding Methods of the Northern Lapps." Sept., 1948.

Voous, K. H., *Atlas of European Birds.* Nelson, 1960.

Vorren, Ørnulv, and Manker, Ernst, *Lapp Life and Customs.* Oxford University Press, 1962.

Vorren, Ørnulv, *Norway North of 65.* George Allen and Unwin, 1961.

Wheelwright, H. W., *A Spring and Summer in Lapland.* Groombridge, 1871.

Wilkinson, Gerald, *Trees in the Wild.* Stephen Hope Books, 1973.

Wilmore, Sylvia Bruce, *Swans of the World.* David and Charles, 1974.

Yonge, C. M., *The Sea Shore.* Collins, 1973.

Acknowledgments

The author and editors of this book wish to thank the following: Skolechef Aarseth, Kautokeino; R. J. Armstrong, Northern Lights Observatory, Tromsø; Edvard K. Barth, Zoological Museum, Oslo University; Tom Browne, London; Roy Carlsen, Kirkenes; Christopher Cooper, London; Philip Cribb, Royal Botanical Gardens, Kew; Charles Dettmer, Thames Ditton, Surrey; Peter Francis, the Open University, Milton Keynes; Randi and Jostein Grastveit, Vadsø; Sally Heathcote, British Museum of Natural History, London; Peter James, British Museum of Natural History, London; Hildur Krog, Botanical Museum, Oslo University; J. R. Laundon, British Museum of Natural History, London; Tony Long, Brede, Sussex; The Librarian, Linnean Society, London; Gunnar Lid, Oslo University; Charles Merullo, London; Dagny Stousland Möller, Judge of Appeal, Oslo; Jens Storm Munch, Tromsø Museum; Sylvie Nickels, Cambridge; Viggo Ree and Petter Schei, Zoological Museum, Oslo University; The Scott Polar Research Institute, Cambridge; Ola Skifte, Curator, Tromsø Museum; Odd M. Smedstad, Fisheries Research Institute, Bergen; Regnor Solbakk, Siida, Kautokeino; The Staff of The Finnish Embassy, London; Glaciology Section, Norges Vassdrages-og Elektrisitetsvesen, Oslo; The Norwegian Embassy, London; Cambridge University Library; Royal Botanical Gardens, Kew; Svein H. Sørensen, Svanvik; Mari Teigmo, De Samiske Samlinger, Karasjok; Kit van Tulleken, London; Turid Uthaug, Siida, Kautokeino; Mikel Utsi, Cambridge; Austin Wormleighton, London; Peter Worsley, University of Reading.

Picture Credits

Sources for the pictures in this book are shown below. Credits for the pictures from left to right are separated by commas; from top to bottom they are separated by dashes.

Cover—Jorma Luhta. Front end papers 1, 2—Kalervo Ojutkangas. Front end paper 3, page 1—Reflejo from Susan Griggs Picture Agency, London. 2, 3—Hans Malmberg from Tiofoto, Stockholm. 4, 5—Stig T. Karlsson from Tiofoto, Stockholm. 6, 7—Edvin Nilsson from Naturfotograferna, Sweden. 8, 9—Kalervo Ojutkangas. 10, 11—Edvin Nilsson from Naturfotograferna, Sweden. 12, 13—Adam Watson. 18, 19—Map by Hunting Surveys Ltd., London. 23—Edvin Nilsson from Naturfotograferna, Sweden. 24—Teuvo Suominen. 25—Jostein Grastveit. 26—*History of Lapland 1674*, by Johannes Shefferus. Courtesy of the Committee of the London Library. 30—Jorma Luhta–P. A. Røstad-Foto, Oslo. 31—Jorma Luhta. 36—René P. Bille. 37—A. Visage from Jacana, Paris. 38, 39—René P. Bille. 40—A. R. McGregor. 41—E. Flipse from World Wildlife Fund, Switzerland. 42, 43—René P. Bille. 47—P. A. Røstad-Foto, Oslo. 50—Dagfinn Skjelle—Jorma Luhta. 51—Edvin Nilsson from Naturfotograferna, Sweden. 55—*Svensk Botanic, 1809*. Eileen Tweedy, courtesy of the Librarian, Royal Botanic Gardens, Kew, Brian Hawkes from Natural History Photographic Agency, Westerham, Kent. 56—*Svensk Botanic, 1809*, Teuvo Suominen. 57—Asko Kaikusalo, *Svensk Botanic, 1809*. 63 to 65—Jane Burton from Bruce Coleman Ltd., London. 66—George Matthews. 67—Jane Burton from Bruce Coleman Ltd., London. 68, 69—Peter James. 73—Dagfinn Skjelle. 77—Hayon from Pitch, Paris. 81—Kalervo Ojutkangas. 85—Edvin Nilsson from Naturfotograferna, Sweden. 89 to 93—*Historia de Gentibus Septentionalibus, 1555*, by Olaus Magnus. By permission of the Syndics of Cambridge University Library. 96—Gösta Andersson. 98—René P. Bille. 100, 101—Kalervo Ojutkangas. 106—Teuvo Suominen. 111 to 121—Toby Molenaar. 125—Dagfinn Skjelle. 127, 129—Jane Burton from Bruce Coleman Ltd., London. 132, 133—A. R. McGregor. 136—René P. Bille. 143—Norman Duerdan from Frank W. Lane, London. 144, 145—Ragnar Frislid. 146, 147—Jostein Grastveit. 148—Jorma Luhta. 149—Gunnar Lid. 150, 151—Viggo Rae. 155—Rob Henderson. 159, 160—Gunnar Lid. 167—D. and K. Urry from Bruce Coleman Ltd., London. 171—Toby Molenaar. 172—Jostein Grastveit. 173—Dagfinn Skjelle. 174, 175—Jostein Grastveit. 176 to 179—Toby Molenaar.

Index

*Numerals in italics indicate a
photograph or drawing of the subject
mentioned.*

Colour reproduction by Printing Developments International Ltd., Leeds, England—a Time Inc. subsidiary.
Filmsetting by C. E. Dawkins (Typesetters) Ltd., London, SE1 1UN,
Printed and bound in Italy (February 1976) by Arnoldo Mondadori, Verona.